WARTIME
FARM

PETER GINN, RUTH GOODMAN & ALEX LANGLANDS

WARTIME FARM

MITCHELL BEAZLEY

CONTENTS

MEET THE FARMERS...

PETER GINN

has swum the Rio Grande during a flash flood, been forced up a pyramid at gun point, avoided the attentions of an illicit antiquities dealer and set fire to himself (twice) – a life in archaeology can throw up many surprises. Having studied at University College London, Peter has a passion for making the past accessible to all. *Wartime Farm* is the latest project in his career of "avoiding a proper job".

RUTH GOODMAN

is an independent scholar and historian, specialising in social and domestic history. She works with a wide range of museums and other academic institutions exploring the past of ordinary people and their activities. Her passion was initially heavily rooted in the 16th century but now sends tendrils out throughout British history. As well as her involvement with the 'Farm' series, Ruth makes frequent appearances on TV's *The One Show*, and *Coast* and in other media.

ALEX LANGLANDS

is an archaeologist and historian with an interest in the landscape and countryside of Britain in the last two millennia. He has worked as an archaeologist on sites all over Europe and has studied farming practices and craft processes from prehistory through to the modern age.

Alex's current area of research is the landscape of early medieval Wessex. He undertakes this from his home on the chalk downland of southern England, and when he is not excavating, researching or writing, he is invariably found in his garden growing food, making baskets and chatting to his bees and chickens.

MANOR FARM, BOTLEY, HAMPSHIRE

» ALEX LANGLANDS

In so many ways, Manor Farm was the ideal place for us to set up as wartime farmers. The buildings and types of livestock were virtually unchanged from the late 1930s, and the location was on the doorstep of the sites where civil defence against possible invasion was organized and the preparations for D-day were made. This, all set against the backdrop of the Blitz in both London and Southampton, meant that we truly were in the hub of wartime England.

THE 21ST-CENTURY FARM

Stumbling across the farm in the 21st century, we found ourselves in a very similar situation to the Warwick family, who bought Manor Farm in September 1941, at a public auction held at the nearby Dolphin Hotel in Botley. The new proprietor, a Mr R Warwick, was charged, as we would be, with improving the farm's output in accordance with Ministry of Agriculture stipulation. The farm had been purchased from the Hammerton family, and both Hammerton boys, Bill and Roy, were kept on as foreman and stockman respectively. Bulking out the workforce was a small team of land girls including Mandy Beaver, Doreen Moon, and Mrs Mucket, and when gangs of labourers were needed for fieldwork, contractors, in the form of gypsies and Italian prisoners of war, were called on to undertake extra work. We, like the Warwicks, would call on the services of the staff at Manor Farm, along with employing a host of other experts and enthusiasts to help us through the year.

As a county, Hampshire is most famous for its rolling chalk downland through which glorious freshwater streams flow. However, Manor Farm sits just outside the chalk and on the heavier clays of south Hampshire and the Solent basin. When the Warwicks purchased Manor Farm it comprised 180 acres of land, and the immediate task, to turn grazing

Right: Manor farm as it is today. Beef cattle, a dairy herd, a host of pigs and a respectable flock of local breeds of sheep make it very much a livestock-orientated farm – as it would have been in 1939.
Below: The farmhouse at Manor Farm as it was in the first quarter of the 20th century.

land over to arable, was to attempt to drain the heavy clay soil so that it could support the growing of cereal crops as part of the war effort.

THE WARTIME FARM

Much of what went on at Manor Farm during the war can be gleaned from the boyhood recollections of Mr R.B.B. Warwick, son of the owner, whose oral history featured as part of an exhibition at the museum at Manor Farm. Back in 1941, the thatched barn where we processed animal feed was once the milking parlour for the dairy herd, and the existing pigsties housed both local Wessex Saddlebacks along with large English Whites. Ferrets for the control of the wild rabbit population were kept, according to Mr Warwick, in the site of the current henhouse, but domestic rabbits were kept as a source of fresh meat. A team of three shire horses would do undertaken the carting and carrying around the farm as well as field work, and occasionally sheep would be brought down from their summer pastures on the chalk hills to overwinter on turnips.

So Manor Farm was typical of a farm as it would have been in the summer of 1939. It was going to be a tantalizing year as we set up shop and embarked on the challenges that the Warwick and Hammerton families had experienced back in the 1940s.

> Manor Farm, as we found it, was typical of a farm as it would have been in the summer of 1939.

HOW IT ALL HAPPENED

» ALEX LANGLANDS

World War II Military

Agriculture and Home Front

1939

16 May 1938: Women's Voluntary Service set up

1 December: National register for war service established

3 June: 20–21-year-old men asked to register for military service

1 September: Blackout begins. Evacuation of children from London begins

2 September: National Service Act enables men of 18–41 to be called up

8 September: Ministry of Food set up under Lord Woolton

September: Petrol rationed

29 September: National Registration Day: ID cards issued

October: 'Dig for Victory' campaign launched

1 September: Germany invades Poland

3 September: Britain and France declare war on Germany

27 September: Poland capitulates to German forces

1940

10 May: Germany invades France and the Low Countries. Neville Chamberlain resigns as Prime Minister of Britain and is replaced by Winston Churchill

27 May–4 June: Evacuation of British Expeditionary Force from Dunkirk

10 June: Italy enters the war allied with Germany

10 July: Battle of Britain begins

7 September: The Blitz begins with a night-long bombing of London

8 January: Bacon, butter and sugar are rationed

11 March: Meat is rationed

14 May: Home Guard formed by Anthony Eden

July: Tea and margarine are rationed

September: Renewed evacuations of children from London

23 September: Southampton heavily bombed

1941

22 January: British army captures Tobruk in North Africa

10 May: House of Commons in London is bombed by the Luftwaffe

22 June: German army begins Operation Barbarossa, the invasion of the Soviet Union

7 December: Japanese air force attacks United States Navy at Pearl Harbor

8 December: Japanese troops invade Malaya, Thailand, the Philippines and Burma

25 December: Hong Kong surrenders to the Japanese army

5 March: Cheese is rationed

17 March: Jams and conserves are rationed

1 June: Clothes and furniture are rationed

4 June: Coal is rationed

18 December: National Service Act (No.2) enables single women aged 20–30 to be conscripted

1942

14 February: British forces identify key German cities as primary and secondary bombing targets

15 February: Singapore is surrendered by the British to the Japanese army

23 April: German air force begins bombing of Britain's historic cities

3 June: Battle of Midway begins between United States and Japanese naval forces

21 June: German Afrika Korps captures Tobruk, North Africa

24 August: German army enters Soviet city of Stalingrad

4 November: British Eighth Army defeats German Afrika Korps at Second Battle of El Alamein

12 November: British Eighth Army recaptures Tobruk, North Africa

January: Rice and dried fruit are rationed; First American GIs land in Britain

9 February: Soap is rationed

6 March: Fuel rationing extended to gas and electricity

12 June: Basic petrol ration withdrawn to be replaced with licences

July: Sweets and chocolate are rationed

August: Biscuits are rationed

1943

18 January: The Luftwaffe renews its bombing of London

13 May: German forces in Tunisia surrender to Allied forces

6 November: Red Army recaptures Kharkov and Kiev

January: Wings for Victory scheme introduced to raise funds for aircraft construction

2 December: 'Bevin Boys' called up for mining work

16 December: Education Bill introduced, paving the way for post-war tripartite system of schools in Education Act 1944

1944

January–April: Heaviest bombing of London since May 1941

4 March: United States Air Force begins bombing Berlin

6 June: D-day landings in Normandy begin

24 August: Allied forces enter Nazi Germany

25 August: Paris liberated

22 January: Coal miners given pay rise to £5 per week

March: Unofficial strikes in mines

21 April: Agreement reached with miners for improved pay and conditions

13 June: First V1 flying bomb lands on Britain

8 September: First V2 flying bomb lands on Britain

September: 'Dim outs' replace 'black outs'

3 December: Home Guard stands down

1945

27 January: Concentration camp at Auschwitz liberated

April: Concentration camps at Buchenwald, Belsen and Dachau liberated

30 April: Adolf Hitler commits suicide

3 May: British army captures Rangoon in Burma from Japanese

7 May: Unconditional surrender of all German forces to the Allies

8 May: Winston Churchill announces Victory in Europe Day

6 August: US air force drops atom bomb on Hiroshima

9 August: US air force drops atom bomb on Nagasaki

15 August: Japan announces its surrender

27 March: Last V2 lands on Britain

29 March: Last V1 lands on London

16 June: Family Allowances Act passed; women receive state payment for first time

18 June: Demobilization of armed forces begins

1948: Foundation of the National Health Service

1954: End of all food rationing

THE BATTLE FOR FOOD

» ALEX LANGLANDS

When we think of Britain's victories in World War II, it is episodes such as the evacuation of the Expeditionary Force from Dunkirk, the Battle of Britain fought in the skies over south-east England, and the D-day landings in Normandy that usually spring to mind. These events are seen as decisive battles, and some argue their significance as turning-points in the war against Nazi Germany. Yet throughout the course of the war, another battle, one without tanks, arms, bombs, or planes, was being fought in the countryside of Britain.

THE FIGHT IN THE FIELDS

This was a battle conducted quietly, with no less courage, in which the stakes were just as high as any fought in the field of combat. For Britain, losing the Battle for Food would have jeopardized the whole war effort and would very likely have led to the capitulation of the British people.

The crux of the problem was that at the outbreak of war, 70 per cent of all food consumed in Britain was imported from abroad. There therefore existed a very real risk of a German U-boat siege creating an impenetrable blockade around our shores and thus cutting the nation off from crucial food supplies. In war there is no greater weapon than hunger, and if Britain were to avoid being starved into submission, it was going to have to, very quickly, make up for the shortfall in foreign imports by battling to produce as much food as possible in its own back yard.

Hitherto, the battle to feed the nation during the crisis of World War II has been largely an ignored topic. When the importance of food supply during this period is considered, it is usually in the context of rationing or the "Dig for Victory" campaign (both covered in detail later in this book). Whilst it may not be at the forefront of World War II histories, it was certainly on the minds of ministers and politicians in the 1930s, as Europe

Right: Ministry of Food propaganda posters encouraged everyone to grow their own food in an attempt to combat shortages and the hardship brought about by the rationing system.
Below: Our ploughing campaign begins in earnest as tired old pasture land was ploughed up so we could plant arable crops.

crept ever closer to war. David Lloyd George, for example, remarked in a speech to the House of Commons on 10 March 1936 that "one of the most important elements in the defence of the realm ... is the provision of food", and as early as 1935 the Minister for Agriculture had set up a committee to consider the problems that another war might bring.

COULD FARMING COPE?

It wasn't going to be easy to transform farming into an industry capable of feeding a population of nearly 50 million people. By 1938, 3.2 per cent of national income was derived from agriculture and fewer than 4 per cent of people worked on the land. Priority was being given to the championing of free trade, the growth of the financial sector and the increase in manufacture to serve a global market. The countryside, with its economic redundancy, had become nothing more than a beautiful rural idyll, to be enjoyed by the masses on long summer weekends. As war broke out, however, it was to rise from this purposeless position to play one of the most important roles in the defeat of Nazi Germany.

DECLINE IN THE INTER-WAR YEARS

The situation encountered in 1939 was not unprecedented and lessons could be learnt from World War I. In 1905-7 the UK imported 75 per cent of its wheat, and it had been a rude awakening for the wartime government

Above: Armies of children were put to work in the fields during the harvest months to help bring in bumper potato crops.

Below: A great emphasis was placed by the Ministry of Agriculture on growing grain cereals such as wheat, oats and barley.

The countryside, with its
economic redundancy,
had become nothing more
than a beautiful rural idyll.

of Herbert Asquith when the German navy began a blockade of British ports in 1914. The reaction had been to pass the Corn Production Act in 1917, which guaranteed prices for wheat and oats and caused, in part, an increase of 1.8 million acres of arable land by the end of World War I. The act was, in effect, a form of protectionism – shielding British farmers from the global free trade against which they were struggling to compete. However, this wasn't to last, and with global peace came a drop in prices. Worse still, in 1920 the world market for wheat collapsed. The government simply could not afford to subsidize British corn growers and on 21 August 1921 the Corn Production Act was repealed. The repeal came to be known among the farming fraternity as "The Great Betrayal", as they were once again left to fend for themselves against the onslaught of cheaper imports. With the high cost of labour and rents, British farmers lacked any real incentives to invest and a period of depression set in.

WHAT COULD BE DONE?

During the Inter-War years there were only a handful of state initiatives designed to improve the farmers' lot. The Marketing Act of 1931 saw the beginnings of organized marketing of produce and the setting up of "marketing boards". Some of these, such as those charged with the sale of milk, hops and potatoes, proved quite successful, and at the outbreak of war, 17 boards had been set up. In terms of arable crops, it was only really in the very niche area of sugar beet farming that the government took interest, sponsoring a number of farmers in East Anglia. In general, however, land originally used for crops was being turned back to pasture for the grazing of dairy cows and other livestock. This trend was most evident in the upland areas of Britain, where crop growing of any kind was all but eradicated in favour of grassland. In the lowlands, there was an added pressure on arable land too, and this came in the form of suburban expansion whereby large tracts of good fertile arable land on city borders were being turned over to the building of new towns and housing estates. Thus, by 1939 arable land had been reduced to two-thirds of what it had been in 1801 and there were two million fewer acres under the plough than there had been in 1914.

It wasn't just arable land that was being lost. The flight of skills and labour from the countryside to better-paid jobs in towns was a situation that had blighted agriculture since the mid-19th century. In the inter-war years, this trend picked up the pace, with a 30 per cent decline in people

Above: Ruth picks the last of the season's runner beans in our productive 'Victory' garden.

The British countryside was to experience an unprecedented level of government involvement.

employed in agriculture since World War I. All round, the figures didn't look good, and in the three years running up to the war British farmers were producing only 30 per cent of the wholesale value of the nation's food. While all the milk and 94 per cent of potatoes consumed were home-grown, only 16 per cent of sugar, oils and fats, 12 per cent of wheat and flour and 9 per cent of butter came from British farms. Furthermore, although 50 per cent of the meat eaten in Britain from 1936 to 1939 came from British-reared stock, a worrying 8.75 million tons of feedstuffs were being imported from abroad to feed it.

THE GOVERNMENT TAKES ACTION

With the example set by World War I most prominent in their minds, the government wasn't going to make the same mistake twice. When it seemed inevitable that Europe was set for a second war, action was taken. The Ministry for Agriculture conducted the Battle for Food on four fronts. Firstly, a ploughing offensive was needed to provide enough land on which to grow the required food. Secondly, the process of mechanization needed accelerating and British farming needed modernizing. Thirdly, labour shortages needed addressing and, finally, an overarching administrative framework was required for the effective running of the campaign.

FAITH IN THE FARMERS

Later in the book we will see how these initiatives took shape. With a raft of incentives and subsidies, the British countryside was to experience an unprecedented level of government involvement. But despite all of this "top-down" action, British farmers still faced an immense task, and the reality was that there remained insufficient labour, skills and machinery to confront the leviathan job that lay ahead. The advice from the War Agricultural Executive Committees was at times lacking in quality and understanding of local conditions, but also the receptiveness of the farming community was found wanting. Remember, many farmers had been burnt by "The Great Betrayal" and, as a consequence, resented government intervention in their affairs. Tales of ministry men requesting farmers to grow alien crops unsuited to the soil without providing them with the equipment and the know-how to do so were common, and it is clear that in places this most unlikely of relationships struggled in its early days. Yet gradually, as the war progressed, communication between both parties improved.

Above: Perhaps the most popular food-related initiative of World War II was the highly successful "Dig for Victory" campaign.

The Ministry of Agriculture found its feet and began to master the level of organization and planning required so that machinery, fertilizers and feedstuffs were finding their way to where they were most needed. Demonstrations of the latest high-input methods were provided on farms in a drive for increased efficiency. Farmers responded not only to the crack of the ministry whip, but also to an emerging prestige and social standing for their position in the community. Playing such an important role in the war effort engendered a level of self-respect that had hitherto been lacking among farmers, and being perceived as fighting on "The Front Line of Freedom" gave them a renewed faith in their calling.

THE FRUITS OF RURAL LABOUR

Unlike conventional warfare, in the Battle for Food there was no clear victory. There was no vanquished opposition and no one point at which the fight was considered over. Ultimately, however, starvation was not an issue for the people of Britain, unlike those in Germany and Russia. And, in that respect, pressure was not placed on the government from a dissenting public struggling to deal with the agony of hunger.

Between 1939 and 1944, 5.6 million acres were added to the total arable area of Great Britain. This represented an increase of 63 per cent and is unique in British agricultural history. Even since, the changes in agriculture we have borne witness to are modest by comparison and the feat seems ever more impressive when we consider the vast developments there have been in agricultural technology since 1945. In the case of the war years, however, it is perhaps wrong to see the technical innovations of the day as the main cause of increased productivity. Some have argued that it is as much down to crude expediency, brute hard work and goodwill as it is to the tractors coming off the production line. The statistics are impressive. Food imports decreased from a pre-war 14.5 million tons to 6 million tons by 1943, and the 63 per cent increase in arable land went someway to making up for the loss of food supply. Of this increase in acreage, the land put down to grain increased by 79 per cent. Perhaps the most telling statistic of all is Keith Murray's calculation in the 1955 agriculture volume of *The History of the Second World War* that the net output of farm products judged in terms of calories rose during the war by 91 per cent. The Battle for Food surely then ended in a resounding victory for the Ministry of Agriculture and those who worked the land.

Below: Peter and I early on in the year. Fresh-faced, enthusiastic, and blissfully unaware of the work that lay ahead

CHAPTER ONE

THE FARM AT WAR

We picked Hampshire as the site for our wartime farm as it is one of the counties that was on the front line of the war. Although the cities took the brunt of the Blitz, it was the countryside that was under threat of invasion, that witnessed the Battle of Britain and was tasked with feeding the nation while playing host to the army and the air force.

During the war, the whole landscape changed. Signposts were altered so only local knowledge could see you right, bunkers were built and barbed wire was laid – all to protect against the Germans who, it was thought, could come from both the sea and (as they had in Holland) from the sky. Every inch of land was precious for producing crops, even hay crops taken from the grassland surrounding airstrips, and those working the land were also manning the battle stations.

Although the invasion never took place, the war against starvation was very real and the largely self-governed rural communities of Britain managed to win it. They ensured that all the mechanical preparations for war were not in vain – an army marches on its stomach, after all, and our army consisted of every man, woman, and child in the British Isles.

THE NATIONAL FARM SURVEY

» ALEX LANGLANDS

In County Circular No. 227, issued in May 1940, the Ministry of Agriculture asked members of the County War Agricultural Executive Committee (CWAEC or "War Ag") to undertake, before the July of that year, a survey of every farm in the country. Described by one commentator as "A New Domesday", the survey was to be even more rigorous than William the Conqueror's survey of England completed 10 years after his defeat of King Harold at the Battle of Hastings in AD1066.

GRADING THE FARMS

The rationale behind the National Farm Survey was obvious. If the Ministry of Agriculture were to increase productivity and eradicate inefficiency across the board, it needed to know the current situation and the areas of British farming where there was scope for improvement.

War Ag personnel were to make a comprehensive evaluation as they set out to designate the appropriate category to each farm. Armed with 6-inch-to-the-mile Ordnance Survey maps, they set out to record every aspect of the farm under inspection. Drainage, fertility and stock-proofing had always been obvious attributes on which to grade farms, but some of the newer technologies, such as water and electricity supplies also came under scrutiny. The condition of agricultural and residential buildings was noted, as were the roads, gates and equipment. Even the level of infestation from rats, rabbits and wood pigeons was taken into account, along with the labour required to run the farm. Upon completion, each farm was given an A, B or C rating. An A-rated farm needed little improvement and was considered to be at or above 80 per cent production. A B-rated farm was hitting between 60 and 80 per cent of its potential productivity, while a C-rated farm, at 60 per cent or below, was in a position where improvements needed to be made.

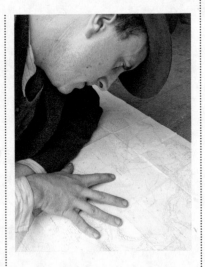

Above: I immediately procured for myself a 1920s copy of the 6-inch-to-the-mile scale Ordnance Survey map to study the layout of the farm in detail.

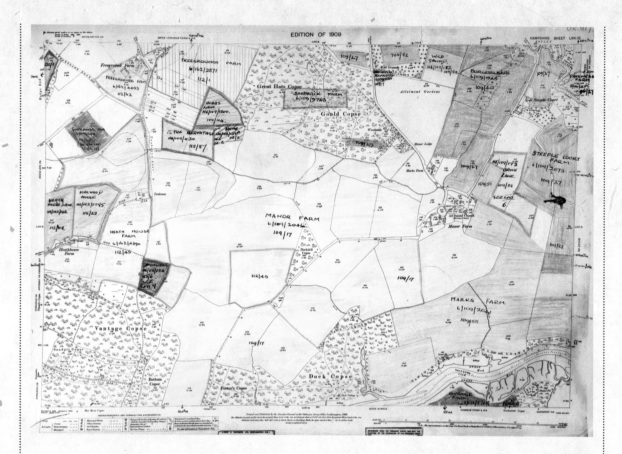

Above: Manor Farm as depicted in the Ministry of Agriculture's own survey records. As part of the National Farm Survey, it was intended that every square inch of the British landscape would be mapped and assessed for productivity.

If the Ministry of Agriculture were to increase productivity and eradicate inefficiency, it needed to know exactly the areas of British farming where there was scope for improvement.

The aim of the survey wasn't necessarily to penalize farmers in the C category – and fewer than 5 per cent of farms nationally fell into this category. It was as much about identifying where a higher level of input, such as with fertilizers and machinery, might result in higher output. The results of the survey put the Ministry of Agriculture in a much better position than it had been in the spring of 1940. Now, it was able to approach the farming community with a greater degree of confidence, to issue orders from a firmer footing and to apply pressure in areas of innovation and improvement that it may have found difficult to do without the facts and figures that the National Farm Survey provided.

THE FARMING COMMUNITY

In fact, one key aspect to the survey was a consideration of the farmer himself. Perhaps one of the most important parts of the survey concerned an evaluation of just how susceptible a farmer might be to embracing change, adopting technological developments and supporting the Ministry in what it was trying to achieve. Much of it ultimately came down to attitude, and it was no longer good enough for farmers to blame low arable productivity and tired pastures on a lack of

FARM SURVEY   17

County: Hampshire   Code No. 6/109/2046
District: 6   Parish: Botley
Name of holding: Manor Farm   Name of farmer: ~~Mary A. Hammerton~~ R. Gwarlock *(her husband)*
Address of farmer: ~~Manor Farm, Botley~~ WICKHAM HANTS.
Number and edition of 6-inch Ordnance Survey Sheet containing farmstead:

A. TENURE.

1. Is occupier tenant ... owner ... — X

2. If tenant, name and address of owner :—

3. Is farmer full time farmer ... X
   part time farmer
   spare time farmer
   hobby farmer
   other type
   Other occupation, if any :—
   Also does work for neighbours

	Yes	No
4. Does farmer occupy other land ?		X

Name of Holding   County   Parish

	Yes	No
5. Has farmer grazing rights over land not occupied by him ?		X

If so, nature of such rights:—

B. CONDITIONS OF FARM.

1. Proportion (%) of Heavy Medium Light Peaty
   area on which soil is 100

2. Is farm conveniently laid out ?	Yes	
	Moderately	
	No	X

3. Proportion (%) of farm which is Good Fair Bad
   naturally 100
4. Situation in regard to road X
5. Situation in regard to railway X
6. Condition of farmhouse X
   Condition of buildings X
7. Condition of farm roads X
8. Condition of fences X
9. Condition of ditches X
10. General condition of field drainage X
11. Condition of cottages X

		No.
12. Number of cottages within farm area		
Number of cottages elsewhere		2
13. Number of cottages let on service tenancy		2

	Yes	No
14. Is there infestation with :—		
rabbits and moles		X
rats and mice	X	
rooks and wood pigeons	X	
other birds		X
insect pests		X
15. Is there heavy infestation with weeds ?		X

If so, kinds of weeds :—

	Yes	No
16. Are there derelict fields ?		X

If so, acreage

Form No. B496/E.I.

C. WATER AND ELECTRICITY.

	Pipe	Well	Roof	Stream	None
Water supply :—					
1. To farmhouse	X				
2. To farm buildings	X				
3. To fields					X

	Yes	No
4. Is there a seasonal shortage of water ?		X

Electricity supply :—
5. Public light
   Public power
   Private light
   Private power
6. Is it used for household purposes ?
   Is it used for farm purposes ?

D. MANAGEMENT.

1. Is farm classified as A, B or C ? B

2. Reasons for B or C :—
   old age
   lack of capital
   personal failings X

If personal failings, details :—

	Good	Fair	Poor	Bad
3. Condition of arable land		X		
4. Condition of pasture		X		

	Adequate	To some extent	Not at all
5. Use of fertilisers on :—			
arable land		X	
grass land		X	

Field information recorded by
P.G.Emery & O.M.Twentyman
Date of recording May 29th 1941

This primary record completed by
P.G.Emery & O.M.Twentyman
Date May 29th 1941

S.F.   MINISTRY OF AGRICULTURE AND FISHERIES   REFERENCE HP 109/17
AGRICULTURAL RETURN, 4th JUNE, 1941,
18th June

LABOUR ON 4th JUNE (Supplementary Questions).

		Number
129	Of the REGULAR workers returned on page 1 (Questions 73—76) how many are :—	If none, please write "NONE"
130	WHOLE TIME FAMILY WORKERS father, mother, son, daughter, brother, sister of occupier or his wife, but not other relations	male / female NONE
131	Of the CASUAL workers returned on page 1 (Questions 77—79) how many are:—	
132	EMPLOYED ON THE HOLDING THROUGHOUT THE YEAR BUT FOR ONLY PART OF THEIR TIME	male / female NONE

MOTIVE POWER ON HOLDING ON 4th JUNE.

FIXED OR PORTABLE ENGINES (Excluding Motor Tractors)	Number in figures	Horse Power of each
		If none, please write "NONE."
133 Water Wheels or Turbines in present use		
134 Water Wheels not in use, but easily repairable		
135 Steam Engines		
136 Gas Engines		
137 Oil or Petrol Engines		
138 Electric Motors		
139 Others (state kinds)		

TRACTORS	Number in figures	Horse Power of each	Make or Model of Tractor
		If none please write "NONE."	
140 Wheel Tractors for field work			
141 Wheel Tractors for stationary work only			
142 Track laying Tractors			

NOTE.—Subject to the special Question No. 134 engines or tractors that have been discarded or worn out should not be included.

RENT

ANNUAL RENT PAYABLE FOR THE HOLDING TO WHICH THIS RETURN RELATES.

		£
143	State the actual rent payable during the current year (i.e., the contract rent less any abatements but including any interest payable on improvements)	
144	If the holding is owned by you, give the best estimate you can of the annual rental value	about 200 £
145	If the holding is partly owned and partly rented by you, state :— Acreage of land which you own and its estimated rental value	Acres £
146	and Acreage of land which you hold as tenant and the rent payable (for definition of rent see Question No. 143)	

LENGTH OF OCCUPATION OF HOLDING. Since the death of my husband 1933

		Years
147	How many years have you been the occupier of the holding to which this Return relates ?	9
148	If you have occupied parts of the holding for different periods, give length of occupation for each Part 1 ... acres ... years Part 2 ... acres ... years Part 3 ... acres ... years	

Signature Mrs S. Hammerton
Address Manor Farm
Botley, Hants

Date 13. Sep. 1941.

The National Farm Survey is rightly considered one of the most innovative of government measures relating to agriculture.

cash or credit because the War Ag personnel came armed with a stock of machinery and expertise to put both B and C category farms on track to higher productivity – if their methods were embraced.

In the most extreme cases, the War Ag could recommend to the Ministry that a farm was requisitioned and placed either directly under their control or in the hands of a tenant farmer of their choosing. In such a situation, there was potential for a huge amount of resentment on the part of the farming community and, of course, the position held by the War Ag could be open to abuse. To have one's farm taken away involved the loss of a livelihood and was resisted by most farmers, especially those whose family had worked the farm for generations. Some War Ag personnel, too, selected from within the ranks of the farming community, were seen to be not so productive themselves on their own farms. For those that had come through the ranks of the agricultural colleges and were without a farm of their own, a requisition might be seen as a convenient way with which to elevate one's status.

Despite these clashes of interest, however, of the 300,000 or so farms surveyed in England and Wales, the Ministry of Agriculture acquired fewer than 1,400 during the war years. Those that fell victim to this fate often did so with the support of the wider local community, and in only a very few instances did attempts to evict farmers result in friction. The main issue for the plaintiff in these cases was that there was no real opportunity for appeal in the whole process. In effect, when a farm was to be requisitioned, the Ministry of Agriculture was perceived as judge, jury and executioner. In defence of this, the Ministry argued that expediency was the key requirement of the day and, in reality, a great deal of leniency was shown by the War Ag towards members of its own community. It should be stressed that the survey was about identifying areas for improvement, not penalizing farmers, and the Ministry had made it clear that help was on hand to achieve greater productivity.

The National Farm Survey is rightly considered one of the most innovative of government measures relating to agriculture. Not only did it allow the government to address the immediate issue of food supply during the war years, but it also had a long-term impact on British farming, as it helped to formulate agricultural policy in post-war planning.

Left: The farm survey for Manor Farm. Section D on sheet 1 was to prove the most controversial part of the survey process, as very often neighbouring farmers and friends had to pass comment on the "personal failings" of their peers.
Below: Peter, Ruth and myself use period tin farmyard toys to help us work out how our farm might have changed during the war years.

GUNFIGHT AT BOROUGH FARM
THE TRAGIC DEATH OF RAY WALDEN

» ALEX LANGLANDS

Very few shots were fired in the battle to increase food production in the British landscape. In one instance, however, the result was the killing of a man and an event that was to shock the Hampshire farming community. George Ray Walden was the tenant farmer at Borough Farm in the Itchen Valley, some 12 miles, as the crow flies, north of our farm at Botley. Ray, as he was known locally, had inherited the tenancy of his farm from his father and it consisted of 62 acres of prime pasture. Good grazing land isn't something that comes about naturally. It takes years, if not generations, to create the even sward of grasses and herbage that provide such excellent fodder for sheep and cattle. It may be for this reason that, in the early months of 1940, Ray Walden rejected the demands of the Hampshire County War Agricultural Executive Committee to plough up 34.3 acres of his pasture for the growing of crops. This decision was to lead, in the summer of 1940, to an 18-hour siege at the hands of the local constabulary, resulting in a gunshot to the head that ultimately killed George Ray Walden.

RISING TENSION

In the short period in the run-up to these events, the Hampshire War Ag had already gained a reputation as a particularly officious bunch, placing, in some cases, unreasonable demands on farmers. Rex Paterson, for example, was a well-respected and innovative dairy farmer. Despite the success he had enjoyed in the pre-war years in milk production, some of the grazing his dairy herd was doing so well on was required to be ploughed up for the planting of potatoes. These famously grow badly in the Hampshire soils, but even so, Paterson, later to be awarded an MBE for his services to agriculture, consented. Ray Walden, however, continued to object and gradually the situation escalated.

Above: Ray's story made front-page reading in the local and national press.
Below: Writer, broadcaster and part-time farmer A. G. Street was inspired by Ray's story to write *Shameful Harvest*, published in 1952.
Right: John Curtis, a boy at the time, of the incident, firmly believes that if the police had allowed his father access to talk to Ray, events might not have ended so tragically.

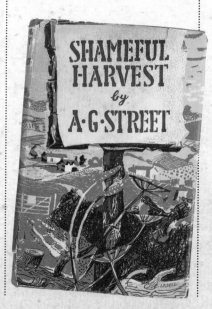

A termination order was placed on his tenancy and when this was ignored, the War Ag had little choice but to mobilize the local constabulary to force the eviction of the disobedient 65-year-old farmer.

At this point, Ray snapped and chose to fight it out until the bitter end. He barricaded himself into his farmhouse and, armed with a double-barrelled shotgun, waited for the police to arrive. Various attempts were made to talk Ray out of the situation he had chosen for himself, but to no avail. It was Ray who fired, seemingly unprovoked, the first shot. With a wounded officer now on their hands, the Hampshire

With a wounded officer now on their hands, the Hampshire constabulary were confronted with what was essentially an attempted murder.

constabulary were confronted with what was essentially an attempted murder. As the siege dragged on into the night, tear gas was used in an attempt to flush the stubborn farmer out by peaceful means. In this instance, a standard issue gas mask came to Ray's aid, but as dawn broke, the decision was made to storm Ray's defensive position. As officers broke into the farmhouse, a volley of shots was fired and, as a consequence, George Ray Walden was mortally wounded.

Ray's case was to prove an inspiration for A. G. Street's book, *Shameful Harvest*. Street was a successful farmer himself and a celebrated writer, and his dedication of the book to Walden reflects the contemporary attitude of some of the farming community towards what was seen as heavy-handedness on behalf of the War Ag. In retrospect, however, it is difficult not to see Ray's death as anything other than a casualty of war and an inevitable consequence of the pressures exerted upon the farming world by a government placed on a war footing.

RECLAIMING THE LAND

» PETER GINN

Britain covers just under 57 million acres and, in order to win the war against starvation, as much of this land as possible had to be turned over to the production of food. The obvious place to start was with the farms, which, since the agrarian heyday of the Victorian period, had seen a decline, becoming a depressed industry in the 1930s. The population had grown, imported goods had increased, farming had declined, derelict ploughs lay in hedgerows, fields were overgrown — and then war broke out. Suddenly this country had to become self-sufficient and that meant cultivating every scrap of land, from farms and fields to parks and verges, to produce food.

The government had two departments relevant to farming: the Ministry of Agriculture, which tried to defend livestock farming, and the Ministry of Food, which emphasized that, acre for acre, crop production for food for humans went further than fodder crops for animals. In 1939, there were 12 million acres of arable land and 17 million acres of permanent grassland. During the first winter of the war, a subsidy of two pounds was given for every acre of grassland that was ploughed. The first target of 2 million acres was reached by April 1940 and by 1944 there were 18 million acres of arable land. Of course, much farm land was lost to the needs of the war: aerodromes and runways, personnel camps, hidden factories. However, the farming community became increasingly inventive about what land it could bring into service, and the war saw farmers navigating their ploughs between the trees in orchards and stealing hay crops from manicured churchyards. Market gardens forsook flowers for the Ministry of Food's favourite vegetable, the potato. Ancient downland hosted the first crops since, in some places, the early Bronze Age, and Windsor Great Park became the largest wheatfield in Britain.

Right: A right royal watering – even Kensington Gardens was turned over to allotments.
Below: Lost? I struggle to find the farm amid the teasles on a patch of land that, during the war, was vital to turn over to arable production.

IMPROVING DRAINAGE FOR CROPS

» PETER GINN

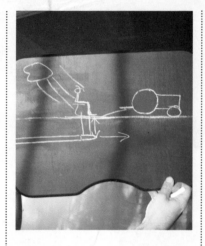

MAKING A MOLE PLOUGH

I would wager that if you were to walk around any farm in Britain, you would see something in the hedgerow or at the back of a barn that is no longer used and has seen better days. Certainly, by the outbreak of war, many ploughs that had been used to turn pasture into arable land had come to be considered museum pieces, and they had to be bought at auction or located on the farm and fixed up. To do this, conversations were had with those who could remember how to set a plough, and craftspeople such as blacksmiths were called out of retirement either to fix existing kit or create bespoke equipment.

Much of the land that the War Ags required farmers to convert to arable was not suitable for the growing of crops, and one of the reasons for this was poor drainage. To drain a field, one can either dig a trench

Above: A diagram of how I imagine the mole plough to work
Below left: Master blacksmith Simon Summers works the fire to forge our mole plough, while also making a cheeky cup of tea.

Above: Simon wrasps the hot iron to clean the surface of impurities.
Above right: Simon, Tom and I midway through the arduous construction.

If a mole plough went through an existing field drain, it would exacerbate the drainage problem rather than abate it.

and install field drains (clay pipes laid in the subsoil that help drain the water away), which is very labour intensive, or one can use a mole plough (also known as a drain plough or subsoiler).

THE SKILL OF THE BLACKSMITH

A mole plough is a bullet-shaped plough that drags through the ground at a depth of around 40cm (16in), leaving in its wake a small channel that will allow water to drain away. They are particularly suited for areas with heavy clay subsoil such as ours, and their use was strongly encouraged by the War Ags. The only problem was that mole ploughs were often used in areas that already had field drains, and if the plough went through the drain, it would exacerbate the drainage problem rather than abate it.

In order to make our mole plough, we called upon the services of Master Blacksmith Simon Summers. He helped me to select the best iron from the scrap pile in the hedge and I helped him to forge it into a new tool through the technique of smith and striking, in which he taps the point he wants to forge with his hammer and I hit that point with the sledge hammer. There is a lot of trust involved in the industrial process of smith and striking in an environment that is purposely kept dark so that the blacksmith can see the colours of the metal. I remain amazed (and quite proud) that I didn't do Simon an injury.

Once we had our plough forged, it was time to use it. This proved more difficult than first anticipated, as the forces placed on the plough underground are immense, so the implement that it is attached to has to be very heavy and therefore unwieldy. It was a steep learning curve as we tried long and hard to make our mole plough work, including bolting it to the heaviest piece of kit we could find, and we came pretty close to success. Throughout the whole process, I did wonder how those wartime farmers coped, as they had to turn their worlds upside down and totally reorganize their farms for the good of the nation.

THE COMING OF MACHINES

» ALEX LANGLANDS

World War II witnessed unprecedented mechanization. Tractors were to radically transform the arable landscape and become a feature of all farms. It was, however, machines like the "gyro-tiller", "prairie-buster", and "rotary cultivator" that would have the most radical impact. Their ability to exploit marsh, hillside, bog, and heath meant the countryside would never look the same again.

THE FORDSON MODEL N TRACTOR, 1929–45

The dreaded day came when I had to meet the farm's new "workhorse"– the Fordson Model N tractor, also known as the Standard Fordson. In much the same way farmers of 1939 would have scratched their heads in bemusement at the tractor, a week into our project, so was I.

The Fordson N tractor built on the success of the Fordson F, a lightweight agricultural vehicle built by American automobile entrepreneur Henry Ford. It became, after its inception in 1916, the first ever mass-produced tractor in the world. British farms were not unfamiliar with Fordson tractors – in 1917, the government had ordered a consignment of 5,000 of the popular Fordson F. Many of these vehicles were still in use in the 1930s but, since British agriculture was in the doldrums in this period, investment in tractors had been minimal. Sensing a potential gap in the British market, in 1928, Ford moved his tractor-producing outfit across the Atlantic. A new factory was planned for Dagenham, Essex, and whilst this was under construction, production was carried out at a Ford plant in Cork, Ireland. Manufacture at the Irish site was problematic, not least because the global depression was in full swing, and production numbers were well below those Ford was used to at his Dearborn factory in Detroit, Michigan. Nonetheless, this hiatus in sales brought positive results, as it gave the company time to work on the product and develop and improve it, ready for when the markets picked up again.

Above: Just over a month into the war, two train loads of Fordson tractors roll off the production line, ready for allocation by the County War Agricultural Executive Committees.
Right: The feats of British farmers are celebrated in the agriculture-themed Lord Mayor's Show of 1947, as a procession of tractors and farm machines are paraded through the City of London. Note the bomb damage on either side of the street.

Most notable among the developments of this period was the fixing of the driver position in relation to the engine. This configuration set the standard and from then on, all tractor manufacturers followed this arrangement. Today, it is unthinkable to envisage any other position than for the driver to be sat between two large wheels with the engine block stretched out ahead of him. Production eventually moved to the intended 66-acre site at Dagenham in 1932, and by 1934 consumers could purchase their tractor with the further innovation of pneumatic tyres fitted as standard, making the Fordson N a versatile beast. Interestingly, the tractors leaving the factory were being painted in the traditional farm cart colours of Essex – a dark blue body with orange wheels.

A MECHANICAL RENAISSANCE

In September 1938, aware that the government was keen to increase home food production, Ford decided to approach the Ministry of Agriculture and strike a deal. On the table they were offering, through government financing, to increase production numbers from 55 tractors per day to 80 per day within three months. This was ultimately deemed by Ford to be of mutual benefit to both parties. Ford was keen to recover after the problems of 1937–8, and the government clearly needed the practical means to carry out its ploughing ambitions in the run-up to war. However, the government's reaction was at first one of caution, even after Ford's second approach in as many weeks. Better late than never, it took until spring of 1939 for the government to change its attitude, as Hitler's actions in Eastern Europe began to sound major alarm bells. This time, it was the Ministry of Agriculture that made the approach to Ford and, by 30 June, a deal was struck wherein production of the Fordson tractor would increase so that 3,000 tractors could be kept in reserve for the time when war broke out.

Fordsons became the most popular tractors of World War II, due to the entrepreneurial foresight of what the Americans did best – mass-production.

Below left: Despite endless tinkering, the Fordson N tractor remained a frustratingly difficult machine to start in the morning.
Below: Ruth very quickly got to grips with the Fordson's clunky and erratic transmission and was soon at ease behind the wheel.

It is essentially for this reason that the bulk of the tractor power on British farms was made up of Fordson Ns. They were by no means the best tractors on the market. At 35 horse power, David Brown's British-made VAK-1 was far more powerful than the Fordson's 28hp, and American imports like the Allis Chalmers B Model with its adjustable wheels was more versatile in that it could do "row-crop" work as well as simple ploughing. By comparison with these and other wartime tractors, the Fordson was difficult to start, temperamental, high on petrol consumption and plagued by a loss of power through an ineffectual transmission system. But, by playing the numbers game, Ford succeeded in dominating the tractor market during the war, with total production numbers from September 1939 to July 1945 reaching 137,483.

KNOWING OUR BEAST

I very quickly grew to despise our tractor. Everything contemporary critics had said about the Fordson was turning out to be true in practice. It was difficult to start, very temperamental, and seriously juicy. After a particularly noisy and smelly afternoon out in the field spent loading sugar beet tops into a cart towed by a Fordson, I was missing more than ever before the quiet and steady reliability of the shire horses I had previously worked with.

Above: Our Fordson N was one of the very early wartime vehicles to come out of Ford's Dagenham plant. We know this because it was painted dark green instead of the characteristic orange. This was because the Dagenham factory had been meticulously camouflaged in dark green paint to make it invisible to German bombers. Clearly, rows of bright orange tractors parked up alongside the factory would give the game away, so the tractors took on the colouring of the factory itself.

NIGHT PLOUGHING

» ALEX LANGLANDS

With the increasing demand for food to be home-grown and a ploughing campaign initiated by the government to meet this obligation, it was clear that farmers and labourers were to spend more time than ever before out in the fields turning over the furrow slice – even if it meant working into the small hours. With the whole of Britain on a war footing, the adoption of shift work became a requirement in many industries. Farming was to be no exception. Under this new regime, we see what might be termed the "militarization" of farming, and slogans like "Ploughing farms is as vital as arms" became commonplace. The plough, once the icon of tranquillity in the countryside, became a weapon of war and the longer it could be wielded in the field, the greater the chance of victory.

THE MECHANICAL HORSE

Farmers could make the most of the advantages tractors gave them over horses. Since the dawn of farming, mankind had been limited by the amount of work their beasts of burden could do, but with the coming of the tractor all of this changed. Now, it was the implement that set the pace and, unlike horses, a tractor needed no rest. In fact, the Fordson N was so troublesome to start that the idea of simply handing it over, still running, so a second shift of operators could work through the night appealed to many farmers.

LIFE magazine reported on 29 April 1940 that, "In every county in England, farmers are ploughing by starlight and by the headlamps of steaming tractors, masked against the sky". We weren't, therefore, going to pass up the opportunity to have a go at this ourselves. We'd read up a little bit on how this was deemed achievable and had placed the requisite lantern in the hedgerow and suitably gilded both tractor and plough with various hurricane lamps. Ruth was to drive the tractor in as straight a line as possible, I was to guide the plough, and Peter was to hover between us to ensure we were keeping as steady a course as we could. In all, we met with a reasonable degree of success, given our collective inexperience and the fact that, despite the ambient glow of the lamps, we were struggling to see anything in the night-time conditions.

IS TWO A BETTER NUMBER THAN ONE?

I'd selected a two-furrow plough because I wanted to make the most of the Fordson's 28hp (most horse-drawn ploughs turn only a single furrow) but this was perhaps a little on the ambitious side. It was heavy and had a complicated lever system by which to set both shares (that is, the cutting implements) at the same depth. As Ruth stayed straight and true in her line, the plough seemed to weave about underfoot on the heavy clay soils and, in my attempts to steer it, the wooden handles that had been subjected to decades of weathering came apart in my hands. I consoled myself that this was something that many farmers in 1939 would have experienced as they pressed back into service ploughs that had not seen useful work since their grandfather's day.

Sadly, we had to call time on our night ploughing and it wasn't till the crack of dawn the next day that I got to assess our handy work. At this point, I began to strongly suspect that the night ploughing I had read about in contemporary magazines and British government-sponsored histories written immediately after the war, was as much a propaganda stunt as an expedient measure. Nonetheless, after my experiences I came to admire even more so those heroes and heroines of the ploughing offensive who had spent so long out in the cold and wet, with only the deafening sound of the tractor engine for company.

THE TRUSTY TRACTOR

» PETER GINN

By the middle of the war, shortages had reached their peak and pressure was increasingly put on farmers to "take their plough around the farm". At one extreme, huge machines such as gyrotillers were being brought in to clear large areas of unkempt land. At the other, much smaller machines such as the Trusty Tractor were being utilized to help convert irregular and random patches of land, such as orchards, roadside verges and the triangles of grass often seen in villages or between fields into usable areas of cultivated soil. Farms such as ours could have hired a Trusty Tractor from the War Ags for a week's use. Trusty Tractors were built between the early 1930s and the 1950s, and the one we used was essentially a single speed 5hp JAP engine running on petrol, driving two wheels with a coupling to which a variety of implements could be fixed.

THE BATTLE OF THE BEAN FIELD

We wanted to sow a crop of broad beans on a patch of wasteland that we had cleared of junk. The beans would fix nitrogen in the soil to improve it for subsequent crops, provide us with a source of protein and allow us to make green manure. To work the land, we started by ploughing it using a swing plough. When Alex got to the end of a furrow and turned the Trusty around, he could touch a lever with his foot and swing the plough so that the up-cast of the next furrow was thrown in the same direction as the first. I stood back and watched, trying to learn from his mistakes (of which there were few). The most important piece of advice we were given was "not to get cocky" and also if it was going to go, then let it go. Although the Trusty looks small, it is very powerful and if it were to catch on a barbed wire fence, it would rip it out of the ground.

After ploughing, I took over for harrowing. We had a set of disc harrows which fitted onto the back of the Trusty. These are basically rotating spades that cut through the earth and work the ploughed soil down to a fine tilth. By adjusting the angle of the harrows, it was possible to adjust amount of soil that was worked. It took a few attempts to get the harrowing angle just right and then it was a case of going up and down and across the field until the required soil texture had been reached.

To control the tractor there are two handles, the right-hand one containing the throttle. Similarly, there are two dogs (levers) that engage each wheel. The throttle was quite sensitive and I found that placing the palm of my hand at the end of the handle and turning the throttle with my fingers gave me quite subtle control. To turn the tractor left or right, you either use your own body weight to swing it around, which is hard but quick, or stop the tractor, disengage one wheel and then execute

Above: One boy's a boy, two boys are half a boy and three boys are no boys at all; our farmers Richard Lowden, Shane Perry and Geoff Ravenhall playing with the Trusty Tractor.
Below: Alex getting to grips with ploughing using the Trusty Tractor.
Right: Alex complains of a "bad back" – this is why. It's harder than it looks.

Given a choice between a Trusty Tractor and a Fordson, I know which one I would pick.

the desired turn before stopping again to re-engage the wheel. When turning, you always have to think about the arc that the handles will take and not attempt a turn too close to a hedge or similar obstacle.

The Trusty was not highly regarded initially, but as they began showing up on farms, a reputation was established. They are versatile and economical and the catalogue comes with adverts for several attachments, including a hedge trimmer. If a match is placed in the throttle, then the tractor will take itself across the field. There are accounts of Trusty Tractors doing the field work while the chaps responsible for turning it around did hedging work. I would have to say given a choice between a Trusty Tractor and a Fordson, I know which one I would pick.

Once the land was worked down, we turned our attention to sowing our crop of beans. Unfortunately we couldn't get our seed drill to work with the size of bean we had, so we ended up sowing by hand. Working the land and hand-sowing the crop was tough work, but our battle wasn't over. As we had been toiling away, we were being watched and when we went for a cup of tea, in swooped the birds, digging in the ground to get at the beans. There is only so much one can do to deter a determined pest. In this case, we opted to cover the land with dead off-cuts of blackthorn bushes. No matter what measures one takes, it is only when the crop begins to grow that you know how successful you were.

HARVESTING CEREAL CROPS

» ALEX LANGLANDS

During our Victorian and Edwardian farming experiences, we had relied heavily on the "reaper-binder" with which to harvest our crops. In the 1880s, this was considered a piece of cutting-edge kit and was so reliable and effective in comparison to earlier methods that, by the Edwardian period, it had yet to be replaced. In fact, well into the late 1930s, this was still the predominant way of bringing in the harvest. The reaper-binder, as its name suggests, did two things. Firstly, it cut the corn in the field and secondly, having passed the cut material through a series of conveyor belts, it bound the plants together in sheaves. These were then spat out the side of the machine for a team of labourers to then "stook" in the field. Prior to this throughout the mid-19th century, cereals were harvested in what can only be described as medieval fashion: by swinging a scythe to cut the plant, bunching the loose stems by hand and tying a sheaf manually.

One job still remained for the farmer and this was to transport the dried sheaves from the field and to thresh out precious grain from the heads of the plant. One of the defining features of the early-20th century rural economy was the flight of labourers from the country to the towns in search of better pay and working conditions. For decades, this, coupled with the cost of paying extra hands, had stimulated the adoption of various methods and machines that could save labour on the farm. The threshing process traditionally required a large team, with as many as 10 men needed to feed the threshing box, keep the steam engine stoked and watered, to bag grain and chaff, and to rick the straw.

COMBINING OPERATIONS

The question was therefore asked by agriculturalists and economists of the inter-war period whether the threshing process could be undertaken in the field at the point of cutting – whether, in fact, a machine could "combine" cutting with threshing. In the late 1920s and 1930s, some innovation in this direction had taken place and companies in both North America and Germany had developed reapers, drawn by tractors, which also had a threshing drum attached. The threshing drum would be powered by a separate engine rather than driven off the ground wheel and this implement came to be known as the "trailer-combine". At the outbreak of war in 1939, however, these implements were rare in North America and Germany, and in Britain they were virtually unheard of.

Left: Elements of the reaper binder can be seen in this forerunner to the modern combine harvester.
Below: An army marches on its stomach, as this poster demonstrates, with the tractor leading the planes into battle.

In the inter-war period the question was asked, could the threshing process be undertaken in the field at the point of cutting?

> Many farms had to make do with equipment that their fathers – and in some cases their grandfathers – had used to cut the crop.

In ordering the British farming community to plough up an extra two million acres of land for the sowing of crops in the spring of 1940, the Ministry of Agriculture had effectively created a huge amount more work at harvest time, with a potentially inadequate fleet of reaper-binders and threshing boxes with which to deal with the surplus. The problem was getting the grain out of the field and into the barn. Many farms had to make do with equipment that their fathers – and in some cases their grandfathers – had used to cut the crop.

BUMPER CROPS

Yields were above average for that first wartime harvest of 1940, due to exceptionally good weather. What's more, further land increases were planned for 1941/42 and, in a twist of fate (that can only suggest the weather was fighting firmly on the Allies' side), Britain had excellent weather conditions for growing and harvesting crops. Severe winter frosts and exceptionally dry springs had unleashed the fertility in the heavy clay soils of lowland England. Well-above average yields were more than a ton per acre for the 2.5 million acres put down to wheat. The reaper-binder fleet was being pushed to its very limits. With the Japanese overrunning Singapore, the Philippines and Burma, supplies of hemp were at an all-time low in Britain. The effective use of a reaper-binder relied on hemp for the binder twine – the cord that bound the sheaves. There was just enough to go round for the 1942 harvest.

Yields were above average for that first wartime harvest of 1940, due to exceptionally good weather.

Left: Combine harvesters helped reduce the amount of labour required to bring in a successful harvest.
Above: Many farms still had to drag out the reaper binder and grease the wheels.
Above right: Our field of wheat. Unlike with modern treated crops there were many weeds, but a thick sowing of seed and good weather and the wheat beat them.

Never before had the demand for combine harvesters been greater and they were very gradually, through the Ministry of Agriculture and local contractor firms, introduced to British farms. By the harvest of 1942, there were over 1,000 in operation. In those early days they weren't without their problems. The main issue was the moisture in the grain they produced. When cut with a reaper-binder, grain could carry on drying in the sheaf stooked in the field. Cut with a combine harvester, the grain goes straight into a sack or storage container and, if it is too moist, risks accelerated deterioration. In North America and Germany, with their hot and dry autumns, this wasn't such a problem. In Britain, the longer you wait for the grain to dry in the field, the closer you get to the inclement weather of late autumn. The skill of the farmer was called into play here, but the government was resigned to further investment in improved storage facilities and grain-dryers. Another problem was that, with so many moving parts, there were an inordinate number of grease nipples to attend to. Forgetting or missing one could result in part failure at a critical point, and spares and servicing were hard to come by.

That said, there could be no doubt about the benefits of combined harvesters for the wartime effort. The Massey Harris 21 stands out as a particularly well-developed and popular combine harvester. Trialled in North America in 1940 and available to buy in 1941, its main advantage was that it was self-propelled. Rather than needing a tractor to tow it around, it could be driven and operated at the same time. This meant more manoeuvrability, whilst at the same time freeing up a tractor for other work on the farm. The cutting bar, too, was placed on the front of the vehicle (instead of a side mounting) and this meant that none of the crop to be harvested would be trampled in the first swathe cut.

GROWING CROPS

» ALEX LANGLANDS

A crop that was to become particularly important during World War II was sugar beet. During the 19th and early 20th centuries, Britain had come to rely on its dominions, in particular those parts of the Empire in tropical climes, for the supply of its raw sugar cane from which to extract refined sugar for the home market.

SUGAR BEET FARMING

The experiences of food shortages during World War I and the risk of being cut off from this sugar supply in any future war led the government to pass the Sugar Beet Act in 1925. The objectives of the act were two-fold. Firstly, a sugar supply needed to be secured and a healthy home-grown industry would go some way to making sure the nation didn't go without in the event of a blockade on imports. Secondly, the government wanted to provide relief to financially depressed arable areas of the country, particularly eastern England, during the 1920s agricultural depression.

This was one of the few interventions made by the government in the agricultural economy during the inter-war years and it led to an enormous increase in the acreage of land set aside for growing sugar beet. Just over 17,000 acres were recorded in 1923, but by 1938 this had risen drastically to over 335,000. The vast majority of this was being grown under contract to the British Sugar Corporation, which operated 18 extraction factories nationwide. The policy of subsidizing the sugar beet industry wasn't without its critics, for during this period it was to cost the British taxpayer some £42 million – money that was going straight to beet manufacturers. But, despite recommendations for an end to the subsidy made by a committee set up to review the situation in 1934, the government decided to continue with the policy, undoubtedly with one eye on Hitler's rise to power. Under the 1936 Sugar Industry

Above: Sugar beet farming was conducted on a huge scale during the war. Daily deliveries at this processing plant added to the already vast mountains of sugar beet awaiting refining.

Right: A propaganda poster from the "Lend a Hand on the Land" series. Sugar beet farming was particularly laborious, requiring many hands at both weeding and harvesting time.

Growing sugar beet needs a lot of labour but it means your household sugar ration

YOUR HELP IS NEEDED NOW

Above: Peter and I marvel at a raw sugar beet. Over 95 per cent of the wartime sugar ration was derived from this peculiarly unattractive vegetable.

(Re-organization) Act, subsidies for the industry became a permanent fixture. When war did break out in 1939, this decision was to pay dividends and the increase in production from 24,000 tons per year in 1924 to 325,000 tons per year in 1938 went some way to making up the nation's weekly sugar ration of 12 oz per person.

TAKING THE "TOPS"

Sugar beet looks and grows very much like a large swede or turnip (although the root is an off-white colour) and it slotted very easily into the British agricultural cycle, taking the place of fodder turnips on which sheep used to graze during the winter months. Sown early in the spring, sugar beet develops a deep taproot that is capable of drawing moisture and nutrients up from the subsoil, making it particularly resilient to drought. Britain has the perfect climate for the growing of this crop and under the right conditions the top of the root grows almost to the size of a human head, above which a large green leafy mass absorbs the sun's rays whilst providing adequate shade for the swelling root below. Because of its wartime significance, Peter and I were keen to find out more about sugar beet farming. We were also in need of some winter fodder for our dairy herd. We visited a farm in Cambridgeshire in the Fens, close to where the last remaining sugar refineries are still in operation, but we hadn't come for the sickly sweet root used to make sugar. We had come for the "tops" – the leafy plant matter that would otherwise get discarded in the process of harvesting.

> Sown early in the spring, sugar beet develops a deep taproot that is capable of drawing moisture and nutrients up from the subsoil, making it a crop particularly resilient to drought.

Traditionally, the harvesting of any beet crop – whether sugar beet, turnips, or swedes – had required a great deal of human labour, so Peter and I were dreading the level of work that might be involved. Each root had to be pulled by hand from the ground, topped and tailed with a special knife and then thrown in the cart. The opportunities for backache and errant finger slicing were many and worrying. However, in the early 20th century, attempts had been made to mechanize harvesting. Fortunately for us, our hosts had managed to acquire, what was in 1930s Britain, state-of-the-art equipment – a "beet harvester"' from Denmark.

A HELPING HAND

The Roeslev beet harvester turned out to be an extremely effective piece of kit. It essentially consisted of two implements coupled together. The first implement "topped" the roots by removing the green leafage from the root with a horizontally set blade. The second implement was the "lifter". By means of a two-pronged fork set diagonally into the earth, it lifted the root to the surface. It was then cast into a large revolving drum to knock as much mud off as possible. Thus, a process that would take hours by hand could be done in a matter of minutes by this marvellous machine. Ingenious. There, lying across the field were rows of discarded tops punctuated by small piles of knocked-clean sugar beet ready for the local refinery. Originally, the tops would be ploughed back in as a green fertilizer but in 1940, with the Ministry of Agriculture keen to promote the use of alternative feedstuffs for livestock, farmers were being encouraged to make silage from such by-products. Having spent half of the day marvelling at the labour-saving qualities of the Roeslev, we weren't going to get away without a little bit of sweat and toil. Pitchforks in hand, we set about collecting up into a tractor-towed cart our quota of negotiated sugar beet tops to take back to Manor Farm.

Above: A Fordson tractor was used to cart the sugar beet tops from the field.
Below left: The Roeslev beet harvester lifted the roots from the ground, topped the leafy plant material and knocked the excess soil from the root before off-loading in neat piles along the field.

FLAX: AN UNFAMILIAR CROP

» PETER GINN

We began to realize quite the level of back-breaking work awaiting us in the harvesting process.

Of the few innovations in cropping during World War II, growing flax in areas where it had previously been unknown was one of the most significant. Flax was grown primarily for its fibres, for use in materials crucial to the military, ranging from tents and cord to parachute harnesses. It was grown under contract to the newly formed Ministry of Supply, a department of the government responsible for ensuring an adequate supply of goods and materials to the three arms of the military.

Before the war, much of our flax had been imported from Northern Europe in its processed form and so, with war imminent, reservations existed about our home-based capacity to grow enough flax to sustain the requirements of our armed forces. In 1939, a mere 4,000 acres of flax were grown in Great Britain, so immediately the Ministry of Supply increased the acreage for the harvest of 1940 to 16,000. Further increases were planned for 1941 to 40,000, and an added 12,000 acres were sought for the harvest of 1942. In each year, though, the Ministry had to work hard to get close to its targets and only reached 15,400 acres in 1940, 32,500 in 1941 and an increase of only 7,000 in 1942. It is not hard to see why the Ministry struggled to convince reluctant farmers that growing flax was a worthwhile enterprise. In the first instance, it was an alien crop to most areas of the country and many farmers had neither the equipment nor the know-how to grow it. Secondly, it was an extremely labour-intensive crop to harvest, with individual plants needing to be pulled manually from the ground. Thirdly, such labour could be ill afforded at a time of the year when the potato harvest was also in full swing. Finally, once the plant had been harvested, dried, and processed, it was extremely difficult to dispose of the by-product, the detritus straw.

THE IMPORTANCE OF FLAX

Most farmers had little choice in the matter if the War Ags decided theirs was the land best suited for the growing of flax. Each county had a quota of acres to meet and, if necessary, compulsory 'Direction Orders' could be issued to force farmers to comply with the Ministry of Supply's demands. These strong measures were an indication of just

Above left: Pouring the flax seed into the hopper of our seed drill.

Left: Flax seed, otherwise known as linseed, could be harvested later, instead of the fibrous stems, to produce linseed oil.

Above: Alex wrestling with the uncompromising steering of our new Field Marshall tractor, whilst I man the seed drill to ensure an even distribution.

how important flax was to the war effort, and so, too, was the fact that, when shortages of artificial fertilizers were experienced, flax was one of the few crops, along with onions, carrots, potatoes, and sugar beet, on which they could be used.

Unlike many of the wartime farmers charged with growing flax, we were actually quite keen to have a crack at growing what we saw as a novel plant. With our wheat crop well on the way, we turned our attentions to growing a flax crop in the adjacent field. To get our crop in the ground, our temperamental tractor pulled a seed drill while we employed the services of working horses to pull the harrow. With a respectable crop maturing in the field, we began to realize the back-breaking work awaiting us in the harvesting process and at that point felt a niggle of regret over our spring-time enthusiasm for planting this unusual and, it has to be acknowledged, quite challenging crop.

Below right: A sheaf of flax plants. Traditionally pulled by hand, flax was notoriously back-breaking to harvest and therefore unpopular with farmers. Flax seeds give us linseed oil, which can be used as a waterproofer, a wood treating agent, and in animal feed.

PROCESSING FLAX FOR FIBRE

From the time of planting, it takes approximately 100 days till the flax plant is ready for harvest, and it will grow to a height of around 120cm (4ft). We had to watch our crop carefully in order to judge the optimum time to get the best quality fibres and the maximum amount of seeds. Harvest too early while the crop is still green and the seeds won't be ready, harvest too late when the plant begins to brown and the fibres will have broken down. We had been told to be on the lookout for a slight yellowing of our plants as a cue to start the harvesting.

Once that stage was reached, we had to mobilize a large workforce. Although flax can be harvested by machine, during the war the crops were largely pulled out by hand, to ensure the root comes too, and this means that the longest possible fibre strands can be obtained. It is for this reason that flax crops were not fertilized, as this would have made

The seeds give us linseed oil, which has an abundance of uses including in the manufacture of linoleum.

the plants too big and too tough to harvest by hand. Once the plant has been painstakingly pulled and threshed for its seed, the long blond "flaxen" fibres are obtained by first retting the plant. This is a process of allowing moisture to seep into the stems so that fermentation can take place as bacteria, aided by the oxygen in the air and the warmth of the sun, react with the damp. This process bursts open the stems and breaks down the outer shell of the plant.

The next process is scutching. This separates the long flax fibres from shorter fibres known as tow (which can be used as upholstery stuffing or, indeed, be carded like wool) and from the waste material in which they are encased, called shive. Once the flax has been separated out, it is heckled, which essentially grades the fibres ready for their various uses. Most of these processes had been carried out by hand for thousands of years but by the time of the war they were all mechanical.

Above, top and right: Yarn, ropes, cigarette papers and teabags are are all made from flax stalks. During the war, the stalks were used for equipment such as parachute harnesses.

PEST CONTROL
THE ENEMIES OF FARMING

» ALEX LANGLANDS

Below left: An infestation of hungry Colorado beetles could quickly make short work of your potato plants.
Right: Many of the pesticides recommended in this Ministry of Agriculture poster have quite rightly been withdrawn from the shelves of gardening and horticultural dealers.

During the depressed inter-war period there was a general ambivalence towards the creatures, fungi and diseases that thrive on farm produce. Rotation of cropping was still being used to prevent the build-up of diseases and insects in the field, but in and around the farmyard, the targeting of rats, mice, squirrels, wood pigeons and sparrows was seen as a time-consuming and relentless pursuit. In many places, such animals became tolerated as part of the furniture of farm life. If the shotgun, farm cat or terrier could pick off the odd offender, that was considered good enough.

During the war years, however, such a situation simply could not be tolerated. Logically, any increase in productivity would result in an increase in pests, and the Ministry of Agriculture made sure that it was prepared for such a scenario by setting up a special department of the War Ag dedicated to the combating of farm pests all year round.

THE COLORADO BEETLE.

GREATLY ENLARGED.

A DANGEROUS FOREIGN POTATO PEST.

In the fields, a whole range of insecticides and pesticides that had been used experimentally before the war were practically applied on a more widespread scale. Whilst undoubtedly helping in the war effort to produce more food, many of the chemicals used back then have since found themselves in the bad books of agriculturalists and environmentalists, so we certainly weren't going to attempt on our farm to use any of the "traditional" war-time pesticides or herbicides.

As far as the wood pigeon was concerned, his aerial threat was considered so dangerous that there are stories that the Royal Observer Corps were called upon to identify some of the larger flocks so that they might be followed and ambushed. Sparrows, although without quite the appetite of the gluttonous pigeon, were nonetheless a serious problem. The Pest Control Staff at the War Ag faced a considerably complex task in reducing their numbers, however. What was to be the secret weapon they devised when the harvest was imminent and the grain in the plant at its most vulnerable? The answer lay in mobs of boys and girls armed with rattles and the ability to shout at the tops of their voices for long periods of the day.

WAR ON RATS

In combating the vermin problem in farm buildings, the War Ag was going to require a much more hands-on approach and a

DEATH TO PESTS

DON'T LET THESE INVADERS RAVAGE YOUR CROPS

THE SIGNS	THE PEST		THE TREATMENT

 SLUG

THE TREATMENT — Destroy with well-mixed "Meta" bait; ¼-oz. with ¾-lb. slightly wet bran broadcast very thinly on soil—3-oz. per square rod — or dot small heaps over affected area.

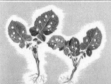 **CABBAGE CATERPILLAR**

THE TREATMENT — Dust plants at *first sign* of damage with Derris dust or spray with Derris insecticide. Repeat immediately more young caterpillars appear.

FLEA BEETLE

THE TREATMENT — Dust seedlings with Derris, Nicotine or Naphthalene dust. Repeat two or three times at intervals of four days.

 **CABBAGE ROOT FLY**

THE TREATMENT — Prevent attack by putting ½ teaspoonful of 4% Calomel dust on soil around each plant as soon as set out. Repeat a fortnight later.

 **BLACK FLY   GREEN FLY   CABBAGE APHIS**

THE TREATMENT — Spray with Derris or Nicotine wash. If sunny and warm, dust with Nicotine dust. Destroy all old cabbage stumps before mid-May.

ISSUED BY THE MINISTRY OF AGRICULTURE

raft of cunning and committed operatives. These were to be found in the ranks of the Women's Land Army, and for each county a small band of dedicated rat catchers were trained and put to work. Having lived on or close to farms for most of my life, I have a personal hatred of rats and wage a constant vendetta against them. I'm a great animal lover but witnessing first hand just how quickly an infestation can do serious damage, I now do everything I can to destroy rats wherever I am. After humans, rats are the most resourceful animal in the world and breed at prolific rates. The level of damage they can do on a farm, if their numbers are not controlled in some way, is immense. Firstly, they have a voracious appetite and 100 rats will easily make short work of a ton of grain. When they have eaten you out of house and home, they start harassing livestock, and it is not unheard of for rats to attack roosting chickens. With their razor-sharp teeth, they will gnaw away at doors and windows, often finding their way into the warmest part of the house to sleep during the day. Finally, their droppings and urine pollute and infect, contaminating drinking water and feed supplies.

So during the war, a new offensive began on farmyard pests. Rabbit warrens were gassed, birds were scared and rodents were poisoned, trapped, and hunted down with ferrets. It was perhaps a sideshow in the greater battle to keep Britain fed, but was nonetheless extremely important.

CHAPTER TWO
MOBILISING PEOPLE

This country was cut off, this country was being bombed day and night, this country was under constant threat of invasion, this country was at war. When we look at society and civilization, we often see structures and the physical impact that humans have had on their surrounding environment. However, it is the people themselves who are important, and it was the ordinary men, women and children that during the war came together in extraordinary ways to create a formidable and unstoppable force.

We had to defend ourselves, we had to feed ourselves, we had to console the bereft and, importantly, we had to keep our spirits up. The impression that resonates from the very soul of this country that existed during the war period is of a people up for the challenge. From the women chopping down trees and loading narrow boats to the ordinary men sent down the mines as "Bevin Boys", and the evacuees transported far from home, everyone did their bit. No matter what problem was thrown up, no matter how massive the trial, these great people found the solution.

POWER
TO
THE
PEOPLE

» RUTH GOODMAN

'We could do with thousands more like you..'

JOIN THE WOMEN'S LAND ARMY

Prior to the agricultural revolutions and modernization of farming, the countryside was teeming with people working on the land. Shortly after the outbreak of war, the demand for labour was back, and we had to call on a number of sources to meet the challenge. Cue the land girls.

LAND GIRLS

When Lady Denman was asked, just before the war, to take charge of the Women's Land Army, she already chaired the National Federation of Women's Institutes and was well known for her practical outdoor approach as well as her excellent organizational skills. The Land Army had first emerged, albeit on a small scale, during World War I. With so many men about to be called on to fight and with a real need to increase the productivity of the land, labour was bound to be an issue on farms. It was hoped that the Land Army would be able to fill some of the gap.

But whilst the government had faith in women as agricultural workers, a lot of farmers were initially highly sceptical. Not only were these young workers female, they were also recruited from the town population. The Land Army was conceived of as additional agricultural labour and so didn't recruit young women from farming backgrounds, who would be helping out anyway, but instead recruited young typists and other girls with no agricultural or even horticultural skills.

The first batch of young women was placed individually on farms, having undergone little or no training. They were expected to learn on the job, and at 18 or 19 years of age many of them were physically small. That farmers gradually came round to the idea is testament indeed to the hard graft and persistence of young women thrown in at the deep end. That is not to say that there were not some who simply couldn't stand it, nor that there weren't difficulties and tensions (sometimes it was

The Land Army recruited young typists and other girls with no agricultural or even horticultural skills.

not the farmers but the farmers' wives who found the girls living in their homes and working with the men so difficult). Some farmers threw the girls out, but in the main the women of the Land Army made a place for themselves as valued members of the agricultural workforce.

After the first few batches were sent out as individuals to live and work on specific farms, it began to be more common to set up Land Army camps where a pool of women lived and could move from farm to farm as a labour gang doing a variety of jobs. A lot of members of the Land Army preferred this arrangement, as it gave them more young female company, and many farmers found it much more useful to have extra labour to deal with gluts of work rather than a single full-time worker.

TAKING ON THE TRACTORS

Tractors were to become a major part of the land girl's work. Driving was a skill in which the Land Army could train its volunteers relatively quickly. The women were sent on both driving and tractor maintenance courses, so when tractors began arriving on farms during the war, it was often the land girls who drove them. The camp and gang system also encouraged tractor driving. Land girls could move not just their labour but also the equipment from farm to farm, maximizing the efficiency of machinery, ploughing first one farmer's fields before moving on to the next. The image of a woman driving a tractor is a wartime icon.

AMELIA KING
PREJUDICE AND PERSISTENCE

» ALEX LANGLANDS

During our research of the Women's Land Army in Hampshire, we came across an interesting story that shed light on the processes by which women came to be accepted and billeted through the Women's Land Army and the County War Agricultural Executive Committees (War Ags). Most importantly, though, Amelia King's story provides a rare insight into attitudes towards people of African-Caribbean British descent in the countryside of wartime Britain. King was a 26-year-old British woman from Branch Road, Stepney, East London, whose father hailed from British Guiana. She volunteered, we are told in coverage in the *Daily Mirror* and *Daily Express*, to join the Women's Land Army, and her story hit the front pages in September 1943. In an interview at the Women's Land Army offices in Oxford Street, London, a female official informed King that finding her a placement would prove difficult because of the objection farmers would have to her "colour". At a later point, she was sent to attend the Stratford Labour Exchange where she was informed that she had ultimately been turned down for the Land Army by the Essex County Committee, so the *Daily Express* reported on 24 September 1943. No apparent reason for this rejection was given and King was offered a job in a munitions factory.

MAKING A STAND
King stood firm and argued that if her "colour" wasn't good enough for the Land Army, then it wasn't good enough for munitions work. Such a stance showed a lot of courage – especially given the climate of the time – on King's part, both to take on the establishment and also to reject the work she had been offered.

The Daily Mirror front page, Friday, September 24, 1943, featuring the headline "5TH IN SIGHT OF DYING CITY OF NAPLES" and the story of Amelia King with the caption "She is British born . . . her father is a merchant seaman . . . her brother is in the Navy . . . but she has been refused work on the land BECAUSE SHE'S COLOURED" and "WLA accuses farmers of imposing bar".

It took a lot of courage on King's part, both to take on the establishment and also to reject the work she had been offered.

There would undoubtedly have been pressure put upon her to avoid creating a "situation", and the consequences of being seen not to contribute to the war effort in the way directed by the authorities were pretty severe. Yet King continued to persist and, after a second attempt to volunteer for the Land Army led to a second refusal and a second offer of munitions work, she took her case to her Member of Parliament, and ex-docker and labour-party member Mr Walter 'Stoker' Edwards.

THE MINISTER

Edwards took Amelia King's case to the Minister for Agriculture, who was, at the time, a man called Mr R. S. Hudson. Whilst being vocal about not endorsing a "colour bar", Hudson is said, by the *Daily Mirror*, to have advised King to volunteer for other work "in view of the extreme difficulties" of finding her employment on the land.

What is interesting here, from the little that can be gleaned from the popular press, is that both in King's first encounter with the Land Army and in Hudson's attitude there seems to be a feeling of powerlessness to combat the prejudice she was facing. Clearly, the female official's instant response at the office in Oxford Street was a consequence of previous and perhaps ongoing cases where young British women of African-

For a healthy, happy job

Join the

WOMEN'S LAND ARMY

stipulation in his area, but also responsible for the billeting of volunteers. He wrote to the papers with an offer of work for Miss Amelia King on his farm in Wickham. King was keen to take up the position, but was insistent on going through the official channels, requesting that, firstly, she should be granted formal membership of the Women's Land Army. On 9 October 1943, the *Daily Express* reported that her request was accepted and King took up her position working alongside an army of 25 other girls on Mr Roberts' farm, close to which four villagers had already offered her accommodation.

Amelia King passed away in 1995 so unfortunately her recollection of the events of September 1943 evades us. However, as an interesting postscript to this tale, we were exceptionally fortunate to track down Mr A. E. Roberts' daughter, Betty. Now in her 90s and living less than a mile away from our farm, Betty recounted in vivid detail Amelia's arrival and her time spent working in and around Wickham. Throughout her ordeal, Amelia King's defiance shines through. She would clearly not be defeated by the faceless prejudice with which she was being confronted and, by demonstrating the courage and spirit it takes to fight such prejudice and discrimination, she was able to contribute to the war effort in the way she rightfully deserved.

Caribbean origin were being turned away by members of the farming community. And Hudson clearly felt, despite his protestations, that he couldn't, for whatever reasons, enforce King's acceptance by the Essex branch of the War Ag. A similar powerlessness is reflected in the Land Army's official statement, issued from their headquarters in Balcombe, Sussex, that despite

doing the best they could, "individual prejudice comes into play sometimes".

The publicity Amelia King's case had garnered attracted the attention of a Mr A. E. Roberts from Wickham in Portsmouth. Roberts was a respected farmer and someone fairly high up in the County Committee responsible not only for overseeing Ministry of Agriculture advice and

Far left: A recruitment poster for the Women's Land Army.

Above: A photo taken during a tea break on Mr Roberts' farm in Wickham. Betty Rudd can be seen sitting immediately behind Amelia (front row).

Left: Betty Rudd today, proudly wearing her Land Army Badge of Honour, awarded in 2008.

LUMBER JILLS

» RUTH GOODMAN

Around 6,000 young women spent a significant part of the war working not with arable crops or livestock, but with wood. Measuring, felling, shifting, and processing the trees of Britain, they turned them into the chestnut "railings" or tracks that were used during the D-day landings, the telegraph poles that maintained vital lines of communication, and the charcoal that created the smokescreen under which the Allies were able to cross the Rhine in 1945. They produced pitprops, ship masts and the beech that was used to construct Mosquito aircraft.

Britain before the war had imported the majority of its wood supply, just as it imported so much else. Any initiative that could reduce this was, of course, important, and a huge national survey of our woodland resources began. The results were promising, but turning that woodland into useable timber required labour. Forestry work was a reserved occupation and throughout the war most timber was produced by male forestry workers. Prisoners of war topped up the numbers, but it was clear that drawing upon female labour would be essential to meet targets.

The Women's Timber Corps (WTC) was formed in April 1942. When local recruitment officially began, the promise of travel, better hours than the regular Women's Land Army, and a more generous pay scale ensured

Above, top: Using a two-handed saw requires rhythm, stamina and a well-matched partnership.
Above: Lifting and shifting was just as much part of the job as felling for wartime lumber Jills. Many chose to do so in customized uniform, like this lively pair – those shorts were originally dungarees!

The trees had to be felled
by a mixture of axe strokes
and two-handed saws.

the Corps was never short of recruits. Girls who joined up were a mixed bunch, with surprisingly few coming from practical backgrounds. Bonny Macadam, who joined in 1942, recalled some of the girls who arrived for training. "There were so many townies – shop assistants, hairdressers ... you name them. They had high heels, hats with veils... absolutely incredible!"

SKILLS OVER STRENGTH

The first few women to find a place in the timber business worked as surveyors and measurers. This was responsible work that required mathematical skills and accuracy. Standing trees had to be measured, their cubic footage worked out, extraction routes planned, stacking grounds organized. Not only was such work vital in planning the logistics, but the pay of the fellers relied upon these measurements. It was no surprise then to find that the first batch of Timber Jills contained a number of university graduates. As the war went on and men began to drift away into the forces, women began to be called on to do the heavier more physical work alongside the remaining men.

Above: After a very satisfying shout of 'timber!', Eve and I got to work with the girls, cleaning up the log and beginning the process of converting it into pit props.

Those who worked as fellers lived a nomadic existence, moving from one patch of trees to the next, living in huts or tents, cycling long distances to outlying areas. There were no chainsaws or cranes. Instead the trees had to be felled by a mixture of axe strokes and two-handed saws. Once the girls had got the tree down, they had to work their way along the trunk, chopping or sawing all the branches off – a job known as snedding – then they had to saw the trunk into the required lengths and lifted them onto the back of a lorry.

It was incredibly physical and skilled work, one of the reasons why small and slightly built people, including women, could do the work. It wasn't all about muscle. You developed muscles undertaking such work, but more important was developing the technique to allow you to handle axes and saws in the most efficient manner, learning how to let the tool do the work, of being clever with leverage and pivot points.

I have watched a lot of men showing off with axes and getting it horribly wrong, unaware of how hard they are making the job for themselves. I am not even close to Lumber Jill standards, but I have done a bit of tree felling over the years, enough to have a real respect for those shop assistants and hairdressers who chopped for Britain.

IDLE WOMEN

In 1943, the Department of War Transport placed an advertisement in several papers for women to join the boatwomen's training scheme. After a six-week course they were to ply the inland waterways ferrying freight from dock to factory and from mine to customer. Those who answered the call were almost all middle-class girls looking for war work that would get them out and about and away from the factories. The IW of their Inland Waterways badges brought forth a sneer from the boatmen who had plied the canals all their lives. It stood for "Idle Women", they said, and the women seized on the name and made it their own.

In a filing cabinet in Berlin languished a document designed to help the German authorities manage a defeated Britain. Its summation of the Inland Waterways system of 1940 was damning. "Despite the favourable natural conditions, the modern waterway system is practically meaningless ... the inland waterways take only 5.4 per cent of all internal traffic." By Northern European standards, 5.4 per cent of freight was small for boat traffic, but it is still a fair old tonnage.

NO CRUISE

In the end, 45 women were employed working the canal boats, shifting coal, steel strip, ingots of aluminium, machine parts, Spitfire components and other heavy goods. They worked in teams of three handling a pair of boats, living in the tiny cabin tucked into one end of one of the boats. The boats had to be loaded and unloaded at each end of the journey, usually without much in the way of lifting gear, and the timetables were punishing. Olga Kevelos recalled working 18- to 20-hour days, week in, week out. Officially the women could take a week's unpaid leave at the end of each three-week round trip, but Olga can't remember anyone actually taking it. It wasn't that the work was as physically taxing as that of some women's war work, but its relentlessness made the life of an Idle Woman hard. There was no privacy and very little space to live in. These were not the comfortably converted holiday homes of the modern canal boat holiday; these were working boats with three people in a space barely six feet square.

In time, a degree of grudging respect did come to the women from the boatmen – the women did the job, and did it well. But the worry always remained that boatmen's jobs and livelihoods were on the line.

Below: Over 5 per cent of all Britain's freight travelled by canal throughout the war.

Right: Wartime canals were no holiday. It was a life of long hours and heavy lifting as cargoes were loaded and unloaded largely by hand, and boats were woman-handled from mine and dock to factory.

You're doing a fine job...

CARRY ON canal workers

These were working boats with three people trying to manage in a space barely six feet square.

WOMEN OF BRITAIN

COME INTO THE FACTORIES

ASK AT ANY EMPLOYMENT EXCHANGE FOR ADVICE AND FULL DETAILS

Left: A female factory worker was triumphant and heroic. Total war needed the support and work of the entire population. For the first time in history, national service became compulsory for women as well as men.

Right: Women proved to be excellent factory workers. Factory owners found them not only to be good at their jobs, but their low pay made them very much cheaper to employ than the men.

DRAFTING WOMEN

In 1943, women were called up compulsorily to serve their country. Huge numbers had volunteered before but this was the first time in history that national service had been extended to women. Germany chose not to call on the labour of its women, turning instead to slavery to fill the gap. It is an argument often put forward that it was Britain's mobilization first voluntarily, and then compulsorily, of the whole population, women as well as men, that gave us an edge. It was an edge that held back the tide till our allies finally got involved – and an edge that carried on allowing us to punch above our weight.

All women from 18 to 40 were to report for war work unless they had children under 14 years of age at home, could show their domestic duties were sufficient to require them to be at home, or were already occupied in recognized war work. As a woman over 40 and already with domestic responsibilities upon a farm, I would not have been called. Just as farming was a reserved occupation for men, farmers' wives were considered to be already engaged in war work. Everyone knew the domestic duties of women on farms included a lot of actual farm work, as well as keeping vital workers clothed and fed. Farmers' daughters, however, were frequently diverted into other work, at a time when factory workers' daughters could be volunteering for the Land Army.

This was the first time in history that national service had been extended to women.

BETTER THAN MEN?

Up and down the country, women were drafted in to do jobs that had previously been reserved for men. They weren't paid as much as the men had been and they had to fight a great deal of prejudice from their male colleagues, but there were very few areas they didn't enter. The manufacturing industry found women to be especially skilled machine operators, much to many people's surprise – including the women themselves. It transpired that many of the premium jobs that men and women had considered to be too hard, physical or technical for women were quite straightforward after all. A girlhood of knitting and sewing had made these women highly dextrous and accurate in their movements. And as I can personally attest, arc welding is very easy in comparison to knitting. Lathes are generally easier to operate than sewing machines, and a day hauling water and doing the laundry develops plenty of muscle for manoeuvring loads around the factory floor.

Driving and vehicle maintenance was another major employer of wartime women's time. Before the war very few women and, frankly, not many more men had been able to drive. It was a skill that only the wealthy or professional drivers could acquire. Private cars were the exception rather than the rule. But since it was a skill that did not require physical strength and had overtones of personal service (think of chauffeurs) this was one area where the authorities thought that women could free up men. All branches of the services trained women as drivers and as motor mechanics. Few senior staff, whether policemen, air force officers or government inspectors, were able to drive, and since they had better things to do with their time than learn how, they needed women drivers.

THE BEVIN BOYS

» ALEX LANGLANDS

Between the wars, the mining industry was in serious decline. When war began, a swathe of disaffected miners left coalmining for jobs in munitions, construction and the armed forces. By early 1941, however, it was becoming apparent that allowing so many miners to desert the industry was an error of the gravest magnitude. Coal production was in free-fall decline, to the point where shortages were likely to seriously affect the war effort. Ernest Bevin, the Minister of Labour and National Service, knew that he needed a minimum of 720,000 miners to produce the 230 millions tons of coal the nation required annually and yet, in 1942 fewer than 700,000 miners were reporting for daily work at the pit. Bevin therefore announced one of the most controversial schemes of World War II. From December 1943, 48,000 conscripts were forced to serve not on the front line but hundreds of feet underground at the coal face.

This wasn't a decision the government took lightly. They had done everything they could to persuade ex-miners, volunteers and new recruits to sign up for a job in coal mining – but with little success. Attracting men to an industry that was famously badly paid and extremely dangerous was never going to be easy, especially considering the superior working conditions and wages in, say, aircraft construction or shipyard work. A particularly harsh winter and the demands that fighting the Germans on a second front might make on national coal production forced Bevin to announce, in a statement to the House of Commons in December 1943, that a ballot would be drawn from the list of registered conscripts and that 1 in 10 would be sent to work in the coal mines.

At first, shock and disbelief swept through the ranks of the first 20,000 "Bevin Boys". Those that had set their hearts on the RAF or the Navy clearly believed a mistake had been made and appealed to the authorities, but in vain. The futility of the appeal system – in reality a sham affair that paid small homage to the legal process – caused widespread anger and dismay. But under the Emergency Powers Act of 1939–41, those refusing to be directed to work down the pits would be liable to a maximum three-month sentence or a fine of no more than £100. Reluctantly, the Bevin Boys accepted their fate, realized they, too, had a duty to King and Country, and set out to their designated colliery.

THE HARSH REALITY OF 1940S COAL MINING

For myself, this was to be a particularly gruelling experience. The Bevin Boys were selected from all walks of life – not just the working classes – and university graduates mixed with technical apprentices and administrative clerks. The situation I found myself in therefore had some

Above: January 1944: the first contingent of Bevin Boys at the Prince of Wales Colliery, Pontefract.

Attracting men to an industry that was famously badly paid and extremely dangerous was never going to be easy.

parallels with those forced to enter the mines in 1944 in that I was not from a traditional mining background. However, there the similarities ended. For my trip, the maximum safety measures were to be in place and it saddens me to have learnt that miner safety was, even in the 20th century, so far down the priority list and that, in fact, during the war the safety record of the industry was to deteriorate.

Bevin Boys were given a paltry six weeks of training. The speed with which Bevin and the war cabinet had made their decision meant that the collieries were simply unprepared for the new intake. Trainers had to be found and sections of mines were needed to be used for training without impacting on production. There was a serious lack of bunkhouses and canteens, especially in the already crowded industrial heartlands. Bath houses, which made the job just about bearable, weren't ready. The Bevin Boys had to foot the bill for their own accommodation, food and laundry – costs that their pay packet just didn't cover.

The scheme was was brought to an end in 1948. No medals were awarded to the conscripted miners. In fact, it was not until 2008 that their contribution to the war effort was officially recognized.

Above: For many Bevin Boys, getting "called up" meant being "sent down". Here a team of lads crowd into a shaft as they wait to descend into Markham Colliery, Derbyshire.

PRISONERS OF WAR

» PETER GINN

In any conflict, there will always be combatant captives, both military and civilian. The Geneva Convention (1st version 1864, 2nd version 1906) laid down rules on warfare, and the 3rd Geneva Convention (1929), written following World War I, specifically relates to the treatment of Prisoners of War (PoWs) from the moment they are captured until their release.

During World War II, Britain played host to largely German and Italian PoWs. Throughout the conflict, only one prisoner escaped and that was German flying ace Franz von Werra. After repeated attempts to slip his guards, he was moved to Canada, from where he escaped to the US in January 1941. He succeeded in leaving America, heading south towards Brazil, before crossing to Spain and on to Italy. Seven months later, and back on active service, his aircraft went missing and he was presumed dead. However, he had already helped the Germans with information on British interrogation techniques, and it was said that his report regarding his treatment improved the treatment of Allied prisoners in Germany.

Below: Conditions were said to be very good for prisoners of war in the UK, however barracks soon gave way to billeting on farms so they could be closer to where they were needed for work.

The Italians were very popular as PoWs. They were originally held in camps and made to do agricultural work (the Geneva Convention forbids any dangerous or military work) but soon they ended up being billeted on the farms themselves and pretty much having free rein. It is at this point in history that Britain gets its first taste en masse of Italian cooking. Pizzas could be fired on brick kilns such as the one we made (see page 212), and the mother of a friend of mine in Dorset would only allow her PoWs to make and dry their pasta on the ceiling clothes airer in front of the range once a week, as otherwise there was too much mess.

Italy famously swapped sides in September 1943 (at which point their PoWs were more popular in the UK than Americans), which is perhaps why the 500,000 German prisoners in Britain who were making up the shortfall of agricultural labourers were never made to work alongside Italians. (The Germans were considered to be the harder workers.)

Ireland was neutral during the war but had its fair share of both Allied and Axis combatants. To deal with them the Irish set up separate open camps for the "prisoners" and allocated each group a local pub.

CONSCIENTIOUS OBJECTORS

The National Service (Armed Forces) Act of 1939 was enacted on the day Britain declared war on Germany and her allies, and it enforced full conscription of males between the ages of 18 and 41. There were a few exemptions, of which one was an individual objecting on the grounds of conscience, either as a pacifist, as in World War I, or for political reasons.

During the period between the wars, attitudes towards "conchies" had changed and the public and the government had become far more accepting of the position. However, it was harder to justify a pacifist position in World War II. A veteran of the pacifist movement of 1914–18, Fenner Brockway, said that he was "too conscious of the evil of Nazism and Fascism to be completely pacifist".

During the first round of conscription, 22 people in every 1,000 objected based on grounds of conscience. In subsequent rounds this number declined. Every one of the 59,192 people who objected (four times as many objectors as in World War I) had to go to tribunal. This resulted in 3,577 people being granted unconditional exemption, 28,720 people being registered as objectors and being assigned to approved work (usually agricultural), 14,691 people registered for non-combative duties in the armed forces, and 12,204 people being turned down. Only three out of every 100 conscientious objectors were sent to prison, compared to 3 in every 10 during World War I, and very rarely did white feathers get sent to 'shirkers' during this conflict.

But an initially tolerant public began to turn upon the objectors as the phoney war gave way to the Blitz and the Battle of Britain during

Above: We had the privilege of meeting Don Sutherland, a wartime conscientious objector (pictured), during the filming of the series. Registered objectors were often assigned to work on farms and were frequently given the dirtiest and most unpleasant of duties. Although he is now 93, Don continues to campaign for peace.

the summer of 1940, with many private employers sacking anyone who had objected. A popular mistake is that a "conchie" is a coward and the reason that they do not wish to go to war is that they simply want to save their own skin. However, it was the bravery demonstrated in the streets by conscientious objectors operating in the civil defence force that helped to temper opinion. Furthermore, a Non-Combatant Corps was established in the army in the spring of 1940, with many members serving in the parachute field ambulances who were among the first to land on the continent during D-day. One German prisoner remarked to his captors that he thought the British were all mad, as he had shot at a parachutist who, rather than returning fire (which would have been hard as he had no gun), asked instead if he had any blankets.

We had the honour of meeting Don Sutherland, who had been registered as an objector during World War II. He had been in Germany shortly before the outbreak of war and had seen Hitler in the flesh and felt the hatred that surrounded him. He had been forced out of his job but had finally ended up on a farm, very much enjoying the essential war work he carried out. Though the thing that resonated the most with me was that his position is not bourne out of World War II, rather it is a

Below and far below: Farms that people had been steadily deserting suddenly had to deal with a huge influx of individuals and families needing a billet.

lifestyle. He continued to object and campaign to this day, because as I write this and as you read these words, someone somewhere is being subjected to the horrors of war.

EVACUEES

During the Munich crisis in 1938 plans were laid down for the mass evacuation of expectant mothers, mothers with small children, the handicapped and, of course, older children. At the outbreak of war, close to four million people were moved from high-risk areas to low-risk areas in an operation seen by the government as a military countermeasure to the inevitable targeting of densely populated areas. This figure was far below the initial predicted numbers, as in reality those that had said they would send their children away opted to keep them at home instead.

Even with the reduced numbers, evacuation had its problems. The mass exodus from cities such as London was billed as a picture of calm and order, but as the trains pulled out of the stations, cracks began to appear. Journeys lasting 12 hours or so were undertaken with no toilet facilities, many children didn't have any food, and the cramped conditions resulted in normally tidy children looking unkempt, and scruffy children looking positively unholy.

At the destination, the logistics of whom to lodge where was a hit-and-miss affair, dependent upon the capabilities of the billeting officer. The City of Cambridge was very organized, with people to meet the trains, and families and school groups being housed together or in close proximity to one another. In other towns, near chaos ensued as children were lined up in a village hall for adults to say, "I'll take that one", or a train expected to be full of children turned out to be a convoy of pregnant women.

Above: For some, evacuation must have been a great adventure. For many, it saved their lives. For most, it must have been heartbreaking. For a few, it must have been a new form of hell.

This would all have been fine had the outbreak of war heralded a wave of bombs in the densely populated areas. However, the phoney war (or "twilight war", as Churchill called it) meant that disgruntled criticism eventually rose to the surface. Had more people been evacuated, then billeting would really have become a problem, with the pseudo-voluntary selection process giving way to a hard line compulsory system that had been predicted to be grossly unpopular. However, evacuation definitely saved lives and for many of the children during the war it was overall a life-enhancing experience.

HARVEST CAMPS

» RUTH GOODMAN

AN EXTRA SOURCE OF WORK POWER

The rural labour shortage worsened as the war continued. Non-conscripted healthy workers increasingly chose building work over backbreaking labour in the fields. Following the contribution of thousands of volunteer farm workers and evacuees during the harvests of 1940 and 1941, the Minister of Agriculture, R. S. Hudson, appealed to the general public to help. In 1943 he announced that more than a thousand harvest camps for adults would be established at which volunteers would spend two weeks (working during the day and being entertained by the Entertainments National Service Association at night) in return for an officially set rate of pay. Recruiting centres were quickly inundated with willing volunteers and employers were encouraged to stagger workers' holidays to allow maximum take-up.

In addition to these adult volunteers, from 1940 harvest camps were also established for urban children and the pupils of public schools. By the summer of 1949, 249 camps housing over 8,000 boys from both public and state schools had been established successfully. Some camps were better organised than others but they all posed enormous logistical challenges, with each 25–30 boys (the ideal camp size) requiring two teachers, two cooks and where the boys didn't do the tasks themselves, up to three camp orderlies to take on domestic duties. Girls occupied separate harvest camps, and farmers reported that they discharged their duties on the land just as well as the boys, if not better. In 1943, over 20,000 girls attended harvest camps and in 1944

Below left: Our harvest camp children were working up an appetite out in the flax field under Alex's instruction.
Below: Cooking facilities on harvest camps were basic, but the food that was produced was always very much appreciated.
Right: The food cooked at harvest camps may not have been the tastiest, but it was designed to provide enough energy to get the workers through the day.

more than 15,000, yet the authorities remained dubious about promoting such camps for girls.

Feeding these young workers proved a mammoth task and students from local catering colleges were encouraged to work as camp cooks, billeted in local houses rather than under canvas. The Board of Education published *Catering for Harvest Camps* and, using this and other Ministry of Food leaflets, such as *Practical Canteen Cooking*, these trainee cooks ensured that the children were well fed and watered.

LOCAL HELP

In addition to harvest-camp workers, rural children were also expected to do their bit to help. As the war progressed it quickly became the norm to take extra time away from school to help with farm work. As well as local schools taking their classes into the woods to gather plants with medicinal value to be passed on to governmental collection schemes, a number of official and unofficial schemes were in place during the early years of the war to use children and undergraduates on farms in term time.

Farmers were full of praise for child workers, often writing to the governing bodies comparing their work favourably with that of adult volunteers. Expecting children to work on farms during term time may have proved controversial, but without such, it is doubtful whether the one million acres of potatoes grown annually between 1941 and 1944 would have been planted, let alone harvested.

Harvest camps proved an enormous logistical challenge, with each needing at least two teachers and two cooks.

CHAPTER THREE
THE HOME AND GARDEN FRONT

My first view of our cottage for the year was a tad disappointing. It seemed, like many rural homes at the outbreak of World War II, to be stuck back in the Victorian era. Agricultural depression left many farming families with little or no money for taking advantage of the many advances in domestic technology that had sprung up during the twenties and thirties.

Large numbers of rural homes were not only outdated but also dilapidated, with even basic maintenance neglected. The National Farm Survey in 1940 paid heed to the fact (see pages 22–5). "Section B Conditions of Farm" included a grading for the farmhouse and cottages alongside one for the farm buildings, fences, drainage and roads. Each could be ranked as good, fair or bad. But just as there was to be a push to improve the condition and efficiency of the farming, so too were there some concerted efforts to make the farmhouses and cottages more efficient and hygienic. In general, this had to be done with very little money, but there were some things that people could and did do regardless.

KITCHENS ARE IMPORTANT

» RUTH GOODMAN

Houses in towns, and especially the rash of new suburban villas and bungalows that spread along the edges of towns in the more prosperous parts of the country, had led the way with a host of new labour-saving technologies. For whilst some areas of the country suffered from atrocious unemployment and hardship, others were doing very nicely. For those, mostly in the south-east, who had work and the chance of a nice new home, there were any number of new products that made cleaning less burdensome and possible for the small middle-class family to manage without servants. Gas and electricity played a large part in this change, of course, but it was by no means the only thing going on in domestic improvements. Easy-clean surfaces and new ideas about organizing space were also enormously influential.

According to *Aunt Kate's Mother's Book*, which was a rather cheap and cheerful partwork housekeeping book of the early 1930s, "easyclean" surfaces and "commonsense grouping" could transform a kitchen, making all "efficiency and economy". Aunt Kate's readers could call upon synthetic marble, imitation tiles, specially varnished thin linoleum, various vitreous products, rubber, oil silks, porcelain and enamel table tops, as well as good old-fashioned washable paint. These products really did make a difference. A surface that can be effectively cleaned just by wiping it down with a cloth rather than by scrubbing is a huge saving of labour. The linoleum floor could be mopped, the enamel worktop could be wiped down, as could the oil silk curtains and tablecloths. Vitreous sinks could be bleached and a new cooker would never need black leading.

As someone who has done her time scrubbing floors, I wanted some of this new easy-clean life. A piece of linoleum upon the floor is not an expensive alteration to a kitchen laid directly on top of the old stone flags, it's a quick job, too. But it was to make a vast difference to my daily life, just as it did for thousands, maybe millions, of wartime women. It may not have been the first thing that jumped into your head when you thought about modernization in the kitchen, but my goodness it is such a practical advancement. Most of the time you don't even have to get down on your hands and knees to clean a lino floor. Use a good long-handled mop, a bucket of soapy water, splosh the mop about vigorously, wring the mop out, rub it over the floor again, throw down a dry cloth and push the very well-wrung mop arouund the floor to leave it clean and dry. You do have to get down on your knees occasionally, of course, to give the corners and tricky bits a blitz, but in comparison, this is nothing.

The "commonsense grouping" has a lot to be said for it too. As well as grouping the sink and cooker closer together to cut out unnecessary walking about, the layout of larder, kitchen cabinet, and work table were also considered, following the "natural order of work". This may seem commonplace kitchen design to us now, but it was a totally new way of thinking about domestic arrangements at the time. Factory-style efficiency was applied to a woman's domestic work. The fewer unnecessary journeys she made, the better, leaving her more time for other tasks or pastimes. How extremely modern it all sounds. We still talk about and desire kitchens that conform to these basic principles – kitchens that are designed to fit us personally, designed to be as easy to use, as easy to clean, as efficient as possible, made to measure, and fitted. Modern kitchens started here.

RUNNING WATER

Sadly, for me, that much transformation was out of the question. We didn't have the time or money to move sinks. But at least I did have a plumbed-in sink, by which I mean that the wastepipe connected the plug hole with a drain. No more carrying buckets of dirty water outside at the end of each job. Now I could just tip it away down the sink. Small advances in technology, making big differences to the workload. A technology doesn't have to be complicated to be hugely beneficial.

We were also blessed with a pump. An indoor water supply – fantastic. The modern suburban home of the late 1930s could expect to have cold running water both in the kitchen and the bathroom. Small boilers (coal- or gas-fired) or electric immersion heaters could be installed to provide

> Linoleum was to make a vast difference to my daily life, just as it did for thousands, maybe millions, of wartime women.

Above: The kitchen cabinet is a miracle of compactness.
Right: Just look at the way the mud and filth lifts off the lino. Being spared the daily floor-scrubbing routine on hands and knees was a true advance in domestic technology, and was more welcome than any gadget would ever be.

some hot running water too. Out in the countryside most people were happy with an indoor pump. I know I was – so much more convenient than having to slog off with a couple of buckets several times a day.

MY MODERN CABINET

Kitchen furniture was undergoing a major change. Let us return to Aunt Kate for her description of improvements on offer. "The kitchen cabinet is a miracle of compactness, combining table, store cupboard, handy drawers and shelves for kitchen utensils. The table part is porcelain topped so that it is excellent for baking ... Ask any housewife how she likes her modern furniture to dust and polish! She will tell you how easy it is to keep with no curlicues and ledges to collect dust."

The all-in-one kitchen cabinet is something of an icon of the age. Replacing the older dressers, they were in fact very much cheaper, manufactured largely from plywood. But they were indeed a good deal easier to clean. With all the shelves now enclosed, dusting really was greatly reduced. My lovely cabinet – my pride and joy – didn't have the porcelain table top described above, but rather an enamelled surface. It is fantastic for making pastry on, cool and smooth. It also incorporates what I can only call a non-refrigerated fridge. This section is divided into three compartments, labelled respectively "bread", "eggs, fats &

Above: Very little new crockery was available during the war. Most people continued to use whatever they already had. This pre-war crockery was actually given to me by my gran.

Left: My non-refrigerated fridge, with its separate sections for bread, dairy produce and meat storage.
Below right: Though admittedly cleaner than coal and quicker to bring up to heat, the paraffin stove was nonetheless a bit of a compromise.

butter, milk" and "meat". A glass front drops down to enclose them. The compartment labelled "meat" has a wire mesh instead of a wooden wall, that's it, no actual cooling element. The mesh is to ensure an air supply without letting the flies in. In reality, keeping flies out is about all it can do, that and being a space that really is very easy to keep scrupulously clean and free from contaminating odours. But every little helps. Having somewhere safe to pop my dairy and meat products rather than having to fashion covers every time just adds that little bit of convenience.

POWERING UP THE COOKER

So, finally, we come to the cooker. Both electric and gas cookers were growing in popularity in the lead up to the war. They were clean to use, with no more hauling buckets of coal through the house, no more dirty

The all-in-one kitchen cabinet is something of an icon of the age.

cinders to rake out, no more coal smuts flying in the air. You didn't need to black lead them, and their flues didn't need attention. They were controllable, even for the novice. The turn of a knob gave you near-instant cooking heat and just as quickly would turn it off. There were a few coal ranges still being manufactured by 1930, but they were the exception rather than the rule. I had rather set my heart on either a gas or an electric cooker. Cleanliness was a massive appeal.

SLAVE TO THE RANGE

I have found that most people who are nostalgic for old coal-fired ranges miss not only their warmth, but also the eternal presence of their mothers slaving away at the things. The women who actually worked them seem to have been only too happy to replace them with a gas or an electric cooker as soon as they could. A coal range means hard, heavy, and dirty work every day. It also ties you to the kitchen. You can leave it for a few hours ticking over, but you have to keep popping back so that it doesn't go out and you have to plan your fire so that it will be ready to cook on when you need it. In short, it is always at the back of your mind and you can so easily feel that it runs your life. If you have no one based at home, ranges become a real nightmare. You have to let them go out during the day and restart the whole thing up when you do get in, which means an hour's wait before you can even boil a kettle. A coal range is a lifestyle rather than a cooker. Women in wartime were increasingly just not in the home all day. There was a desire to be free from the ties of the range, to be able to pop home after work and get the dinner on in minutes, to be able to turn it off and leave the house without worrying about the fire being alight – let alone enjoy all the time saved by a cooker that didn't need cleaning out and black leading daily. It is no surprise that people were trying to switch over to electricity and gas.

NEW POWER SUPPLIES

Most of the modest new homes springing up in the suburbs had gas or electric right from the beginning. Gas and electricity companies competed for the cooker market, with gaudy adverts and special offers. Patchy electricity supplies had given the gas suppliers a bit of a lead in the 1920s, but in 1926 the Electricity (Supply) Act established a Central Electricity Board that was up and running by 1933. However, despite being called a national grid, it didn't run everywhere. Connecting up the rural population was slow and patchy.

When the war started, the government, too, was trying to encourage the move. Coal was going to be a scarce resource in wartime. Even before war broke out, we knew that we were going to need all we could mine to keep the factories, trains, and engines of war moving.

Like many countryside dwellers I found that the services which towns people had come to take for granted were simply not available.

Above and top: Small Lister D-type generators provided electricity in the countryside. Lighting and milking machines could be run by such engines but, sadly cookers could not.
Right: Light came to the sheds, too, where Peter installed a string of lights run off the same generator.

House coal would be in competition with this need. Although much electricity was powered by coal-fired power stations, it was still felt that less coal would be used domestically if more people used electric appliances. Government advice was to switch. Adverts throughout the war played upon this approved status. "Electric Cooking Wages War On Waste!" ran one strapline. "Electric cooking is extraordinarily clean – and cheap. It costs only about 1 unit per person per day. Go to your Electricity Showrooms for free and friendly information and for help in your wartime kitchen and cooking problems."

NOT ENOUGH JUICE

But I couldn't. Much though I would have liked to, I could not switch over to gas or electricity, as there was no supply of either to the farm. Like many countryside dwellers, I found that the services that townspeople had come to take for granted were simply not available. When I was first told the sad truth, I had hopes that a generator would be the answer to my national grid problems. The milking shed already had a small Lister D-type generator, which powered the milking machine – one of the main reasons that we retained our milking herd. But no such luck. The national grid in 1939 ran on AC current at 132 kV (50 Hz), which was plenty for powering cookers. But the generators produced DC current at much lower voltages, sufficient for a milking machine or a string of lights, but not powerful enough for a cooker.

COOKING ON PARAFFIN

Another form of cooker that I had not considered until that point, was paraffin. Not really a new technology, just a newish use of an old and very simple technology. In essence, the paraffin stove was just a tin box placed over a paraffin lamp or two. But it did have some of the

advantages of the electric and gas cookers: cleanliness, controllability, and cheapness which were all trumpeted in their adverts. When they arrived, the stoves seemed awfully flimsy. In some ways that, too, was an advantage. They needed no installation or even any special stands. They simply rested on a table, which I tucked into the old fireplace where the range had been. I filled the lamps with paraffin, lit them, and away I went. It couldn't have been easier really.

I soon discovered the drawback, however. They never truly got piping hot, and it took quite some time to get a sizzle going. I was going to have to learn a good range of simmering recipes. The oven would be good for baked potatoes, but struggle to bake bread. Ah well, you live and learn. At least I wasn't raking out cold ashes every morning.

SHEDDING LIGHT ON LIGHTING

Although I was not to have an electric cooker, I could make use of electricity in the home in other ways. Lighting for a start. It is so easy to take this simple technology for granted and not notice what an enormous impact it has upon daily life. Advice on how and where to site your new electric lights abounds in household manuals of the day, pointing out how new this was for most people.

Electric light means that you can work after dark. It may seem an obvious thing to say, but it has to be remembered that candles and oil lamps only give enough light for jobs that don't require great precision. Even gas lamps can be a bit on the dim side. Having electric light in the home meant that you could extend the working day and not have to plan jobs around the light levels. During the war, when everyone's workload inevitably rose, those extra hours were very welcome. Not so much

> Whilst not exactly new in 1939, the radio was to be a wartime lifeline, linking the nation together.

Left: Electric irons were one of the most popular of the new electric domestic appliances.
Above right: Electric light allowed us all to work much longer hours.
Right: Nothing perhaps is more evocative of wartime Britain than the radio broadcasts, whether they are of news, music or comedy.

labour saving – although it has to be said electric lights don't need the wick trimming and glass cleaning of the old oil lamps – but labour enabling. The electric light was to give us a lot of flexibility.

LIFE-CHANGING GADGETS

If my talk about my new modern kitchen seems a little light on gadgets, then you will be pleased to know that I did have one at least. An electric iron. This was the most popular of all the new electric gizmos both in the 1930s and during the war years themselves. It plugged into the light socket – wall sockets didn't arrive till much later in most homes – and would run happily off the generator. Just as well really, as I think I might have had trouble heating up my old flat irons on the new paraffin stove. This was clean, quick and easy. The clean part was especially welcome – there was no danger of smearing black smuts all over my washing.

And finally, of course, I mustn't forget to mention the radio. Whilst not exactly new in 1939, the radio was to be a wartime lifeline, linking the nation together with an intimacy and immediacy that transformed every part of life. It was to bring information, consolation, news, distraction, calls to action, and membership of a modern nation at war.

LAUNDRY AND HOUSEWORK

» RUTH GOODMAN

Wartime cleaning presented a range of challenges, each calling for ingenuity as well as hard work. Soap rationing certainly didn't make things easy. The ration consisted of four units per month – or one a week per person. For this one unit, you could purchase either a 4oz bar of hard soap suitable for scrubbing floors and household cleaning, or a 3oz bar of toilet soap suitable for washing people. Or you could choose to use your unit to buy 6oz of soft soap, generally used for washing up and similar tasks, or you could have between 6 and 12oz of soap powder (the amount depended on the amount of actual soap involved), which most people used for general laundry. Another option was 3oz of soap flakes, mostly used for laundering woollen fabrics, or you could expend your unit on liquid soap.

LAUNDRY RATIONS

Since the ration was only one unit per person per week, it was necessary to come up with a soap plan. If you used a whole 3oz bar of toilet soap a week to wash yourself and your hair (a 3oz bar is really quite small), that would leave you with no household cleaning products and nothing to wash your clothes in. Daily showering and hair washing would easily use up that 3oz bar within the week. Think of how many cleaning products you have for the home, all of which replace the soap and scouring powder of wartime. Add them up and see how much soap in one form or another you really use. That one unit per week had a lot to do.

Sensibly, the ration comprised four units per month, rather than one per week, which allowed you to purchase a mix of different types of soap for different purposes, even though the total volume is the same.

Shaving soap was not rationed, the need to hang on to social mores and traditions overriding the practical in this area, just as it did with lipstick for women. Shaving soap could also be used for personal hygiene since,

Top: A familiar brand; but in a much smaller quantity. The laundry powder came in 3oz packets – enough for just one washday.

Above: Hard soap was also used to wash clothes as well as being used for other household cleaning tasks. Not a sliver was thrown away.

Right: Using a mangle is a highly efficient (and physically tiring!) way to remove excess water from your laundry, and speeds up the drying process. You had to be careful to wrap any buttons within the folds of the clothes you pushed through your mangle or they would be quickly crushed to pieces.

RESOURCEFUL CLEANING TIPS

Wartime women were advised to use alternative cleaning products, and a resourceful woman could find ways of cleaning just about everything around the home without using any soap, leaving her with enough for washing and laundry. A soap-free home can still be a clean one, and a few household items that were regularly used included:

Salt: for scrubbing wooden work surfaces

Vinegar: used in a weak solution for wiping enamel and formica worktops; for washing up glasses, cups and saucers; for cleaning paintwork

Splash of milk: for polishing linoleum floors

Bicarbonate of soda: for all kinds of stain removal

Damp newspaper: used in a screwed-up handful for cleaning windows, and wiping out greasy pots and pans

Whiting: mixed with a tiny amount of water, used as a scouring powder for cleaning baths, sinks, pots and pans

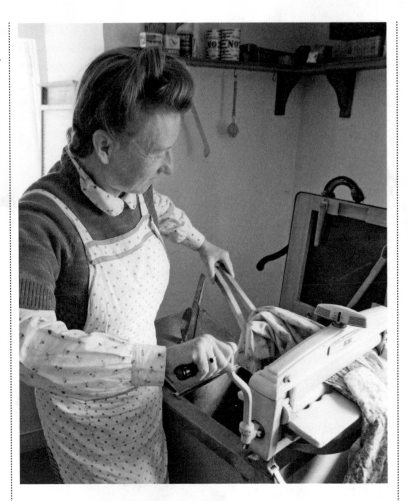

like toilet soap, it was sufficiently fat-rich not to do too much damage to skin – unlike the fat-poor, but alkali-rich, cleaning soaps.

SOAP SAVERS

The last tiny slivers of any bar could be put in a jar with warm water and turned into a jelly that was excellent for washing up or soaking woollen clothes. A small square of flannel placed beneath the soap on the wash basin would pick up enough residue for an additional wash or two. Borax and salt helped soap to go further, especially in hard-water areas. And in addition, there were also a host of tips about cleaning without any soap at all. The wise housewife returned to older ways of keeping her home and family clean, ways that had been in common use before the advertising campaigns of the soap manufacturers had made the twenties and thirties woman so very soap orientated. Salt, borax, vinegar, bicarbonate of soda, and various scouring powders came back into their own and the household manuals of past generations were dusted off .

A resourceful woman could find ways of cleaning just about everything without any soap, leaving her with enough for washing up and laundry. But even here there were a few old tricks that helped. Only the greasiest of pans and dishes really needed soap; glasses, cups and saucers and lightly soiled plates can be washed up just as thoroughly with our old friend the splash of vinegar – indeed, glasses are better done this way. A screwed-up handful of damp newspaper can remove most of the grease from a pan before it goes in the washing-up bowl, reducing further the amount of soap you need. If there are any suds left at the end of the washing up, you have flushed some of your hard-earned cash down the plug hole.

NEW TECHNOLOGIES

There was also the challenge of new materials. Aluminium, celluloid, vulcanite, Bakelite, asbestos, Formica, chromium plating, electroplating, rubber, rayon, and nylon were appearing in homes up and down the country in myriad forms. All of these new materials needed to be cleaned – get it wrong and you could ruin them. The wartime housewife also had to get to grips with the maintenance of new technology: how to wire a plug, how to change a light bulb or fuse, how to change a washer and when to call the gas man were all skills in which she had to become proficient – it was no use being a stick-in-the-mud. Electricity, too, brought its own new dimension to household cleaning. Sockets and switches, cables, and flexes require certain handling. So whilst much wartime household advice was a matter of picking grandma's brains, there was also a large body of new information and skills a woman needed.

SPECIALIST CLEANING

Chromium-plated items were not to be cleaned with soap, and neither were electroplated goods. For chromium, paraffin was recommended, just a little on a soft cloth to clean and bring back the shine. For electroplated items warm water with ammonia did the job although a rub with a little cigar ash could be used as a polish if available. Aluminium pans blackened if you used harsh alkali soap or washing soda on them (the best method was acidic vinegar and water), whilst enamelled pans could be kept from scorching by cutting a circle of asbestos and popping it beneath the pan.

New clothing fabrics also required different care from the old cottons and woollens. These were so easy to ruin that several of the government *Make Do and Mend* leaflets dealt with the best ways to launder and iron them. "How to Look after Rayon" , advice leaflet no.6, tells you to dip and squeeze your rayon clothes, never to rub them or wring them out. Dirt, the leaflet tells us, is unable to penetrate the fibres of rayon and sits on the surface, so rubbing and wringing are not necessary. If you felt tempted to use vigorous washing methods, rayon would distort and

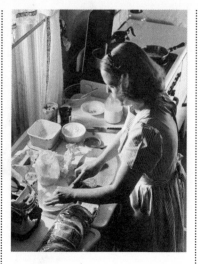

ISSUED BY THE BOARD OF TRADE

2 good tips about rayon
from Mrs. SEW-and-SEW

CAREFUL WASHING MEANS LONGER WEAR! Rayon only soils on the surface so dirt will come away easily if you squeeze it gently in warm lather and rinse well; hard rubbing and bleaching are unnecessary. Squeeze out excess water, pull gently into shape and hang evenly over line. Very hot water, undissolved soap and rough rubbing can do more harm to your rayons than the actual wear and tear of daily use.

SIMPLE RULES FOR IRONING. Iron on the wrong side still slightly damp with a moderately warm iron, gently pulling the garment into shape as you do so. Do not sprinkle with water and avoid pressing over fasteners, buttons and seams.

 free leaflet . . . *with full information on how to look after your rayons, including mending and 'Make-Do' suggestions. Send a card to the Public Relations Dept., Board of Trade, Millbank, London, S.W.1, asking for the Rayon Leaflet. Free and post free.*

JOIN A CLASS. Your local Evening Institute, Technical College or Women's Organisation is probably running a Make-Do and Mend Class. Ask at your Citizens' Advice Bureau.

Above left: New materials and equipment all required new types of cleaning and maintenance. A wartime housewife needed to keep up with the times.

Left: Laundering man-made fibres was a new skill. Get it wrong and that precious last pair of stockings could be ruined.

Above: Despite the introduction of new fabrics, cotton sheets and woollen blankets were still the norm and we found that they kept us cool in summer and warm in winter.

break, although the leaflet failed to say that, since the government was keen to encourage its use to ease pressure on cotton and wool supplies.

RESHAPE WHILST DAMP

To dry rayon articles, the leaflet recommends rolling them in an old towel before hanging them up to dry to remove excess water. This was important as the weight of the water could also distort the clothes' shape. Rayon dresses were not to be pegged to the line, but draped over to minimize the drag. Rayon stockings were to be rinsed in warm water daily and hung by the toes to dry. When it came to ironing there was further danger. People usually used only a very hot iron, as they were accustomed to ironing cotton and linen. The advice leaflets returned to this subject again and again – they call for only a warm iron, tested on a sheet of paper to ensure that you don't scorch or melt the material.

Later on parachute nylon made it into the shops. This was the first nylon available in Britain, and didn't have all the advantages that were promised for nylon designed for clothing. Nonetheless it was both new and available, so a lot of underwear was made from it. People needed all the advice they could get on how to launder it. Unlike rayon it could be rubbed to remove dirt, but not wrung out. In fact it dried very easily, but distorted equally easily if hung up to dry.

HOMEMADE TOOLS

The need to make do and mend extended to all branches of wartime life. Just like pretty much all other areas of manufacture, factories that had once produced household implements were turned instead to producing for the war effort. So when things wore out in our wartime kitchen, we had to find ways of making replacements ourselves out of whatever we had to hand. In this, as in much else, a farming family did have resources that were unavailable to many in the population at large.

Many people kept a few chickens, both in the town and countryside. In common with other farming folk, we found that we had too many at the outbreak of war. Those birds that were surplus were sent to slaughter. This gave us something of a bonanza of feathers, which I was determined not to waste. Some went in my quilt (see pages 208–9) but I had some spare.

A CHICKEN FEATHER DUSTER

Before the war, feather dusters had been imported from South Africa, and made of ostrich feathers. I couldn't find any detailed wartime instructions on how to make up the duster, just a note or two to say that it would be a good idea, so I largely had to invent it for myself, based on a bit of flower arranging and arrow-making experience (yes, I know most people don't make arrows in their spare time, but I am somewhat history orientated.) This is my method:

1 FInd a suitable stick and take the long tail feathers from several birds – chicken feathers work well.

2 Wax a long length of thread to strengthen it and prevent it from snapping or fraying.

3 Bind a bunch of five or six feathers together by themselves with the thread first and tightly bind that bunch to the top of the stick.

When things wore out in our wartime kitchen, we had to find ways of making replacements out of whatever we had to hand.

4 Bind the remaining feathers to the stick by winding the thread down and placing feather after feather against the stick as you go, each new turn of the thread binding them tight. I knotted the thread against itself at intervals so that if it were to snap in the future it would only unwind a few turns and not the whole way down.

The duster worked very well, and I haven't lost any feathers off it yet.

MAKING A MOP

When it came to replacing my mop, I followed a tip I had found in *Farmer's Weekly*. We had an old broom whose bristles had largely worn away, so I scouted around for as much old rag as I could find. This I folded into a thick pad, which I then wrapped around and nailed on to the broom head. It only took a few minutes and it did the trick nicely, although it is much heavier to use than the purpose-made mop that it replaced.

Left: My chicken feather duster in action – very easy to make if you are practised at fletching your own arrows!.
Right: Rags, a worn-out broom and a few tacks made a serviceable mop.

THE GARDEN FRONT

» RUTH GOODMAN

When we first arrived at Manor Farm, I was delighted to see that there was already a good-sized garden in full operation. Rows of runner beans were dripping with pods, bushy lines of beetroot, carrots, and parsnips were in evidence, and the soil around them was well-turned, fertile-looking stuff. The other side of the path was a deep flowerbed rioting with colour. I looked on with admiration, but also a tinge of sadness. The flowers would have to go.

DIGGING FOR VICTORY

Flower gardens were a luxury that wartime Britain could not afford. Good garden soil like that needed to be growing vegetables if we were to get through the war with full bellies. As government information made clear right from the start, farmers would no longer be supplying Britain with vegetables as they had done. Market gardening concerns were being turned over to arable production. As it said on one of the earliest Dig for Victory posters "Women! Farmers can't grow all your vegetables. You must grow your own. Farmers are growing more of the essential crops – potatoes, corn for your bread, and food for the cows. It's up to you to provide the vegetables that are vital to your children's health".

Even before the slogan "Dig for Victory" had been coined, the Ministry of Agriculture was issuing gardening advice to the general population. "Food From The Garden" was the first of the Growmore bulletins issued in October 1939, in a collaboration between the Royal Horticultural Society (RHS) and the Ministry of Agriculture. The Ministry of Agriculture had also harnessed the help of a popular radio gardener, Mr C. H. Middleton, or "The Wireless Gardener". Middleton's Sunday afternoon radio broadcasts continued throughout the war, playing to enormous audiences. One of the secrets of Middleton's success was the friendly

Above: Mud and Peter go together like Strawberries and Cream!. I was only too glad to have a bit of help in the garden now and again.
Below: 'Dig for Victory' was one of the most important campaigns on the home front.

Your own vegetables all the year round . . . if you

DIG FOR VICTORY NOW

Above: The flowers growing when we arrived would have to go; the Minister of Agriculture in 1940 appealed to every householder to convert flowerbeds to vegetable plots.

"These are critical times, but we shall get through them, and the harder we dig for victory, the sooner the roses will be with us." Mr C. H. Middleton, "The Wireless Gardener".

tone of his broadcasts; the weather in Middleton's garden was usually poor, the pests usually plentiful and very hungry, but it was his advice that helped millions to get the most out of their gardens.

GROWING ON EVERY INCH OF LAND

Through advice such as that given by Mr Middleton, people were encouraged to dig up every available scrap of land and grow food upon it. Aerial photographs taken during the war show just how thoroughly people took this to heart. Not only were front and back gardens dug up, but roadside verges and railway cuttings, public parks, school playing fields, even the moat at the Tower of London.

We were glad to get any food I could grow out of the garden, but I also knew full well that wartime neighbours would have been very disapproving of any garden ground going to waste. If I were to dig up all the flower beds, I should have a vast area, along with the vegetable plot. This was more than I felt I could manage by myself alongside all the other wartime work I knew I would have. So taking inspiration from the pig club (see pages 118-21) I decided to see if there was anyone locally who would like a bit of garden space, someone who didn't have access to much land. We could work the area together and share the produce.

YEAR-ROUND CROPS

Just like today, there was always plenty to do in a wartime garden. There were bean seeds to collect for next year's crop, young beetroot plants to thin, onions to pull, dry and store, and the broad bean patch to dig over. There was a good supply of parsnips and beetroot already growing, which could be harvested in the coming months but, when we arrived, I noticed the winter greens had not gone in. We were going to be short.

Summer gluts followed by winter scarcity were a problem early in the war, as new gardeners grew summer crops but were inadequately covered for the winter. Advice from the RHS came thick and fast to gardeners, prioritizing a style of vegetable gardening that gave a reliable year-round food supply, and the Ministry of Agriculture published a cropping plan for winter vegetables (see right). The plan also detailed sowing and cropping times, and information on planting distances.

PLANNING AND PLANTING

Such a succession of veg required careful planning and sequential planting. The first of my broad bean seeds had gone in in late November, their hardy shoots overwintering though not growing much. As February came to a close, a second sowing of broad bean seeds went in. These were only about two weeks behind my November-sown beans when it came to harvesting them. Further sowings of beans went in at two-week intervals. A similar plan (though without the overwintering) followed for most other types of vegetables, so that we could continue to spread out the harvests of each one. Fast-growing catch crops were grown between slower-growing ones to add variety to the garden's produce. These crops included salad plants, such as lettuce and spring onions.

Above left: With the flowers gone, the garden begins to get into its productive stride.

Above: Wartime recipes are full of parsley, so I made sure I planted a good long row.

Right: The Ministry of Agriculture published this leaflet showing a cropping plan for winter vegetables, The reverse showed cropping times and planting distances.

Summer gluts followed by winter scarcity were a problem early in the war for new gardeners.

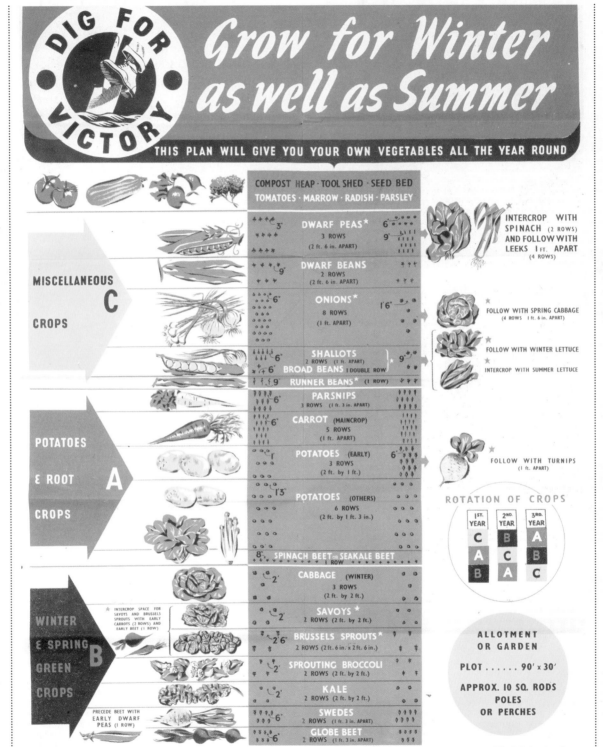

DIG FOR VICTORY

Grow for Winter as well as Summer

THIS PLAN WILL GIVE YOU YOUR OWN VEGETABLES ALL THE YEAR ROUND

COMPOST HEAP · TOOL SHED · SEED BED
TOMATOES · MARROW · RADISH · PARSLEY

MISCELLANEOUS CROPS C

DWARF PEAS*
3 ROWS
(2 ft. 6 in. APART)

INTERCROP WITH SPINACH (2 ROWS) AND FOLLOW WITH LEEKS 1 ft. APART (4 ROWS)

DWARF BEANS
2 ROWS
(2 ft. 6 in. APART)

ONIONS*
8 ROWS
(1 ft. APART)

FOLLOW WITH SPRING CABBAGE
(4 ROWS 1 ft. 6 in. APART)

SHALLOTS 2 ROWS (1 ft. APART)
BROAD BEANS 1 DOUBLE ROW
RUNNER BEANS* (1 ROW)

FOLLOW WITH WINTER LETTUCE

INTERCROP WITH SUMMER LETTUCE

PARSNIPS
3 ROWS (1 ft. 3 in. APART)

CARROT (MAINCROP)
5 ROWS
(1 ft. APART)

POTATOES & ROOT CROPS A

POTATOES (EARLY)
3 ROWS
(2 ft. by 1 ft.)

FOLLOW WITH TURNIPS
(1 ft. APART)

POTATOES (OTHERS)
6 ROWS
(2 ft. by 1 ft. 3 in.)

ROTATION OF CROPS

1ST. YEAR	2ND. YEAR	3RD. YEAR
C	B	A
A	C	B
B	A	C

SPINACH BEET OR SEAKALE BEET
1 ROW

CABBAGE (WINTER)
3 ROWS
(2 ft. by 2 ft.)

WINTER & SPRING GREEN CROPS B

INTERCROP SPACE FOR SAVOYS AND BRUSSELS SPROUTS WITH EARLY CARROTS (2 ROWS) AND EARLY BEET (1 ROW)

SAVOYS *
2 ROWS (2 ft. by 2 ft.)

BRUSSELS SPROUTS*
2 ROWS (2 ft. 6 in. x 2 ft. 6 in.)

SPROUTING BROCCOLI
2 ROWS (2 ft. by 2 ft.)

KALE
2 ROWS (2 ft. by 2 ft.)

ALLOTMENT OR GARDEN

PLOT . . . . . . 90' x 30'

APPROX. 10 SQ. RODS POLES OR PERCHES

PRECEDE BEET WITH EARLY DWARF PEAS (1 ROW)

SWEDES
2 ROWS (1 ft. 3 in. APART)

GLOBE BEET
2 ROWS (1 ft. 3 in. APART)

ASK FOR COPY OF PLAN AND 'DIG FOR VICTORY' LEAFLET No. 1 or write for free copies to Ministry of Agriculture, 55 Whitehall, London, S.W.1.

ROUTINE TASKS

Many of the problems faced by wartime gardeners are the same as those that gardeners face today, such as staying on top of weeding and controlling pests. Thankfully, we are not confronted with the dangers of enemy action, which saw many clearing broken glass from shattered greenhouses, and don't have to deal with oil or the release of pests in boxes dropped onto fields from German planes. In the Ministry of Agriculture's *Allotment & Garden Guide*, published in January 1945, the wartime gardener's constant battle against pests is obvious. Children were often enlisted to collect cabbage white butterflies and caterpillars, while in the farmyard ever-helpful poultry were encouraged to eat slugs and snails. During the war and in the years following victory, it was a matter of duty to keep weeds down, and where weeds were in danger of encroaching on someone else's property, a fine could be levied.

GATHERING SEEDS

In the spirit of making the garden's crops go as far as possible, the wartime gardener would have gathered seeds for the next year's crops. However, *Allotment & Garden Guide* gave the following advice, "The only 'safe' vegetables for seed saving by the amateur are peas, beans, onions, leeks, tomatoes, lettuce, ridge cucumbers and marrows." And it wasn't sufficient just to gather seeds from the last of your crops, as these would not give you the best results the following year. The Ministry's advice was to plan your seed gathering when your crops were at their best in July. "One good lettuce plant should give you all the seed you will need." But it was vital that the wartime gardener regarded the plant they chose to keep for seed as being at least as important (or even more so) than any they would choose to eat, monitoring them closely as they grew for any signs of disease. And timing for gathering was equally important and required similar vigilance, "with lettuces, as soon as you see little tufts of fluff forming on the seed heads, pick them and put them in a shallow cardboard box or a seed box with a sheet of paper on the bottom". Rainy weather required a different technique altogether and, of course, you only got one chance to harvest. It may not have been worth gathering tomato seed unless you have an enormous glut as," at least 10lb of tomatoes are required to produce 1oz of seed".

HARVESTING AND STORING

So, with the harvest in full swing, if gathering seeds wasn't always the best way to ensure you had fresh vegetables, what else could you do to extend your crops? Carrots could be stored inside in boxes, sandwiched between layers of dry sand, soil or ashes, or outdoors in clamps, again protected from the cold by sand and straw and then, finally, with around

Top: Keeping on top of the weeding was essential..

Above: Harvesting food from the garden is always a very satisfying task.

TABLE OF PLANTING AND PERIOD OF USE
WINTER SUPPLIES PRINTED IN GREEN

| CROP | TIME OF SOWING | DISTANCE APART | | PERIOD OF USE |
		Rows	Plants	
BEANS (Broad)	Feb.–March	1 double row	6 in. by 9 in.	July
BEANS (Dwarf)	Late April–Early May	2½ ft.	9 in.	July–Aug.
BEANS (Dry Haricot) ..	Late April–Early May	2½ ft.	9 in.	Winter
BEANS (Runner)	Mid–May		9 in.	July–Oct.
BEET	(1) April (2) June	15 in.	6 in. (thin)	July–April
BROCCOLI (Sprouting) ..	Mid–May Plant Mid–July	2 ft.	2 ft.	April–May
BRUSSELS SPROUTS ..	March Plant May–June	2½ ft.	2½ ft.	Nov.–Mar.
CABBAGE (Spring) ..	July–August Plant Sept.–Early Oct.	1½ ft.	1½ ft.	April–Jan.
CABBAGE (Winter) ..	Mid–May Plant Mid–July	2 ft.	2 ft.	
CABBAGE (Cold Districts)	April	1½ ft.	1½ ft.	Autumn
CARROTS (Early) ..	April	1 ft.	6 in. (thin)	June–Sept.
CARROTS (Maincrop) ..	June–Early July	1 ft.	6 in. (thin)	Oct.–May
KALE	May Plant Mid–July	2 ft.	2 ft.	Jan.–April
LEEKS	March Plant July	1 ft.	6 in. 9 in.	Mar.–May
LETTUCE (Summer) ..	March and every 14 days	Between other crops	9 in.	May–Oct.
LETTUCE (Winter Hardy) ..	Sept.	1 ft.	9 in.	Spring
MARROW	May		3–4 ft.	July–Feb.
ONIONS	Mid.–Feb.	1 ft.	6 in. (thin)	July–June
PARSNIPS	Mid.–Feb.–Mid.–March	15 in.	6 in. (thin)	Nov.–Mar.
PEAS (Early) ..	March and April	2½ ft.	3 in.	June–July
PEAS (Others) ..				
POTATOES (Early) ..	March	2 ft.	1 ft.	July–Aug.
POTATOES (Others) ..	April	2 ft.	1 ft. 3 in.	Sept.–Mar.
RADISHES..	March onwards	1 ft.		May–June
SAVOY	Late May Plant July–Aug.	2 ft.	2 ft.	Jan.–Mar.
SHALLOTS	February	1 ft.	6 in.	Jan.–Dec.
SPINACH (Summer) ..	Mid.–April	1 ft.	6 in. (thin)	Summer
SPINACH (Winter) ..	Sept.	1 ft.	6 in. (thin)	Spring
SPINACH BEET .. or SEAKALE BEET ..	April	8 in.	8 in. (groups)	July–Oct. Jan.–June
SWEDES	End June	15 in.	6 in. (thin)	Dec.–Mar.
TOMATOES	Plant end May		15 in.	Aug.–Oct.
TURNIP (Roots)	July	1 ft.	6 in. (thin)	Oct.–Mar.
TURNIP (Tops)	End August	1 ft.	Sow thinly	April

20cm (8in) of soil on top. Beetroots needed to be lifted before there was any danger of frost, with the leaves twisted off and the roots buried in boxes or barrels of only moderately dry sand and then stored in a shed, cellar or other frostproof storeroom. If frost threatened, an extra layer of old sacks, bracken, or straw could be piled on top of the storage boxes. If this was done properly, the roots would keep for several months. Onions had to be completely dry before being stored, and it was advised that their roots should be loosened and the onions hung on ropes in a dry place with good air circulation. Marrows and pumpkins were hung in nets from the ceiling or stored singly on shelves. In this way, they could be kept until the following January or February.

Above left: Charts such as this helped people to plan their planting so that there would be vegetables on the table all year round..

HERBS AND SALAD

Growing your own herbs was a sensible way of enlivening the rationed diet. With so many spices proving scarce, a well-stocked herb garden could make wartime meals much more pleasant. Looking at recipes published during the war, a small list of essential herbs comes to the fore. Parsley, sage, thyme, bay leaves, chives and mint are often mentioned, in very much that order of priority, with parsley being the king of all. Indeed, if you are to follow wartime cookery, you will need a *lot* of parsley. The Ministry of Agriculture's leaflets give surprisingly little information on growing herbs but they do tell gardeners to sow parsley in March and then again in July for succession growing. A wartime herb garden was likely to have a large patch of parsley, a couple of vigorous sage bushes, a thyme plant, a few chives along the edge and a patch of mint. Most people used dried bay leaves rather than growing their own.

As we had plenty of space, we decided to be a bit more adventurous, although we did make sure we planted lots of parsley. It is tricky to germinate, but once it comes up, parsley is a very easy herb to grow. It works particularly well among the vegetables, liking the same sort of soil conditions as carrots, and being a strong-smelling plant, it helps to distract the carrot root fly. The sage bushes along the edge of what had been flowerbeds were allowed to stay, and around them we popped in thyme, chives, sorrel, winter savory, rosemary and a bay tree cutting. The mint we grew in a large container, as untrammelled it can spread like wildfire.

GROWING YOUR OWN TOMATOES

This was actively encouraged, as tomatoes have high nutritional value and only a few simple rules needed to be followed for a successful crop:

- Tomatoes need rich fertile soil, but no more than 10cm (4in) deep.
- If planted out in the garden, tomato plants can suffer from cold winds, and in cooler years they can fail to ripen. However, potted up next to a south-facing wall, they will yield a much earlier and more abundant crop.
- If grown in a container, there must be an adequate drainage hole in the bottom or the plants will drown, as roots need air as well as water.
- Soil can be dug from the garden but it needs to be well manured.
- Chicken or rabbit dung mixed in water makes an excellent feed.
- For support, push canes or sticks into the soil next to the plants. Against a wall, stretch some wires along the wall to tie the plants in.
- Painting a wall white before you grow tomatoes against it will allow heat to be reflected onto your plants and will encourage growth.
- Pick the fruit in the late evening or early morning, and leave them in a cool place for 12 hours before eating.
- Tomatoes are ideal for preserving, as they can be bottled whole or used as a sauce, as well as being a great ingredient for chutneys.

Top: Salads were enthusiastically promoted during the war and helped the rationed foods go further.
Above: Collecting and preparing medicinal herbs for the pharmaceutical industry provided a source of income and a way of helping with the war effort.
Right: 1 Chives. **2** Sage. **3** Comfrey. **4** Purple Sage. **5** Collecting marjoram. **6** Apple mint. **7** Wild garlic. **8** Thyme. **9** Parsley.

HOME REMEDIES
NATURE'S MEDICINE CABINET

» RUTH GOODMAN

Before the war, around 90 per cent of plants used in medicinal drugs in Britain had come from abroad, so the sourcing of effective home-grown versions was therefore another priority for the countryside. Many useful drug-yielding plants grow wild in this country, and others can be cultivated in our climate. Some of these are still in use, but in the 1940s we used a wider array of native plant-based drugs than now. Foxgloves provided the digitalis for heart drugs, whilst we looked to deadly nightshade and henbane for atropine, hyoscyamine and hyoscine. These are dangerous substances and those who collect and process them have to be accurate. Under the aegis of the National Herb Committees, and aided by the Women's Institute, pickers were carefully trained in plant recognition.

GATHERING ROSEHIPS

Other medicinal plants, however, are both milder and safer, and the workforce here can, and did, include children. Rosehips gathered from the hedgerows were my father's main source of childhood income during the war. The local distillery converted part of its processing equipment so that hips could be turned into rosehip syrup. This has a very high natural concentration of vitamin C and was given to babies and small children when oranges were in short supply. Rosehips are easy to identify in the hedgerows and cannot be

mistaken for anything poisonous or dangerous, so they were a good subject for country children to collect. The going rate for deseeded hips was 2d per lb, but taking the seeds out is both tricky and messy, so my father, along with many of the other children, settled for the 1d per pound rate offered by the distillery for whole hips. Collected in paper bags that had a habit of disintegrating at awkward moments, spilling the scratchily won harvest, they were just one of a sequence of wild harvests that he and thousands of other children brought in. About 20 different plant species were collected and processed on a large scale across the country, helping to ease the country's medicinal supply lines.

KITCHEN CURES

Many people still swapped hints and tips on homemade remedies that kept down the cost of illness in those pre-National Health Service days. Raw onion juice and sugar for sore throats was one. Cut an onion into rings, sprinkle with a teaspoon of sugar and allow to stand. It will "weep" a juice that was widely held to be both a soother for sore throats and something that could prevent you from catching a cold.

ANCIENT BELIEFS

Stinging nettle, which was a useful additional wartime, vegetable, was also widely touted as a good "blood cleanser and tonic" in the spring. Mustard chest plasters

turn up surprisingly often in people's accounts of wartime life –surprising because this is an old medieval cure for chest complaints, based upon the idea of drawing out the cold wet phlegm humour through the skin to its humoral opposite, the hot, dry-natured mustard. Its persistence as a home remedy right through to the middle of the 20th century is remarkable, and testimony

to how little contact with the medical profession most people could afford. Many families had their own minor medical traditions. In mine it was hot water, whisky and sugar; not exactly herbal, but trusted for pretty much everything.

Many useful drug-yielding plants grow wild in this country, and others can be cultivated in our climate.

CHAPTER FOUR

WARTIME FOOD

Rationing had been resorted to before; in 1918, the government had been forced to step in as food supplies became critical at the latter end of World War I. With so much of our food being imported, it was clear that cutting those supply lines and starving us out would be a major enemy strategy during another war.

The 48 million inhabitants of Britain could not be fed entirely from within these shores, and economic pressures during the twenties and thirties had served to increase further the reliance on imported foodstuffs. Nor could it be said that imported foods were just luxuries.

Flour and fats were mostly imported, with very small amounts being home grown; about half of all meat was imported, along with about three-quarters of the sugar we used. These were the staples of the British diet, with flour for bread being particularly important.

FOOD RATIONING

» RUTH GOODMAN

The farmers were trying to grow more, and production was switched to those crops that yielded the most food value per acre for the population, but there were still going to be major shortfalls. Many shipments of food would continue to get through, but with the demands for armaments and industrial supplies, troop ships and other military requirements there would be fewer ships dedicated to food transport, even without the concerted efforts of the German navy.

Above: The sugar ration varied from 1lb per person per week at its most generous down to half that at other times. Pretty tough if you have a sweet tooth.

Below: The meagre cooking fat ration tried the ingenuity of every family cook.

IMPORTANCE OF FAIRNESS

Leaving the poor to starve whilst the rich ate was not going to be an option. If we were to win the war, we needed the whole population – young men to fight and everyone else to support them with arms, ammunition, uniforms, and food. Even the most right wing of capitalists, who had been perfectly content to leave a generation of workers and their families unemployed, malnourished and desperate in places such as Jarrow during the 1930s, saw the need to feed the whole population now. Malnutrition and starvation would not win the war. What food there was had to be maximized in its potential to keep as many people as possible in good health.

EQUALITY FOR ALL

Rationing seemed the only option. It would prevent waste, it would offer the best possible nutritional levels across the entire population, and it would offer a feeling of fairness. The fairness was important, and became increasingly so as the war progressed. As the war effort demanded more and more effort from people, often with longer working hours in harsher conditions, that feeling of fairness, of being "all in it together" was to be a major tool in getting people to cooperate. Fairness with food was the lynchpin of much that we like to call "the Blitz spirit" of wartime Britain. The rich might well find rationing hard and restrictive, but to the poor it had a whole different character. The twenties and thirties had seen pockets of really terrible poverty in the older industrial areas. To the hungry men, women and children who subsisted largely on bread, jam and tea, the ration looked highly inviting – 4oz of bacon a week. Each. Imagine being able to afford that!

That, of course, brings us to an important point – rationed food was not distributed free – you had to pay for it. The ration was not an entitlement as such; it was a limit on the amount you could buy. Having carefully calculated the nutritional needs of the population to the best scientific knowledge of the day and allocated resources accordingly, the food planners were keen that everyone should eat their entire ration and gain the maximum health benefits from this carefully balanced scheme. But it still came down to money for many.

MORE FOOD FOR THE RICH

Wartime wages helped a lot of people increase their standard of living since most family members were likely to be in work. Unemployment was a thing of the past, making it possible to afford something closer to the level of rationing. But for quite large numbers of people, war work still failed to raise them to a level at which they could afford to buy their entire ration. Whilst the wealthy carped about the privations of rationing, there was still a substantial group who lived below that level of provision. There were, however, ways in which rationing itself could help with this. Illegal though it was, you could always sell elements of your ration. The easiest way was through an understanding – or profiteering, depending on your viewpoint – shopkeeper. Say that you could not afford to spend more than a shilling on meat this week, but your ration entitlement was one shilling and ten pence. You could give the butcher the whole of your meat coupons, all 1/10d, in exchange for a discount, meaning that you actually received, say, 1/4d worth of meat for your 1s of money. The shopkeeper could use the extra coupons to obtain larger supplies next time he went to the wholesaler and sell the surplus on the black market at a nicely inflated price. It gave the poorer person a chance to eat better than they could ever have afforded before and the wealthy person the opportunity to top up their ration a little further.

Leaving the poor to starve whilst the rich ate was not going to be an option.

Above: Working out how to feed a family was a constant worry and challenge, especially as the ration kept on changing. As meat was allocated by price, you could either choose a large amount of cheaper cuts (as seen in the parcel in the background) or a smaller amount of good cuts (see foreground).

A PRE-RATIONING MEAL

Everyone over 25 years of age at the outbreak of World War II entered wartime with strong recollections of life in World War I. The memory of food shortages was sharp and vivid. We knew as a nation what we were facing: that imported foodstuffs would all too soon disappear from the shelves, that even basics could well be in short supply before too long, that real hunger was a serious possibility.

My own father recalls being taken by his grandmother to the market to buy a banana, so that he would remember what one was. She knew that it would be the last he saw till the war was over.

In the late summer of 1939, everyone knew that war was imminent. Looking through pre-war cookery books, I thought it would be a good idea to have one last peacetime meal of our own. Like my great-grandmother, I wanted to take a moment to say goodbye to the banana.

Flicking through my copy of *The Modern Housewife's Book*, my eye was caught by a page of "quickly made dishes for busy days" with two banana-based dishes, and over the page a pineapple candlesticks recipe. Between them they seemed to include just about everything you would struggle to get in wartime Britain, including lemons and glacé cherries.

BACON AND BANANAS

6 bananas
4 tablespoons butter
1 tablespoon lemon juice
6 tomatoes
12 bacon slices
fried bread

1 Peel the bananas and brush them with a little melted fat. Fry lightly in the butter along with the lemon juice and tomatoes. Remove to a hot dish, then crisply fry the bacon and some croutons of bread. Arrange the bananas, tomatoes and croutons around the bacon to serve.

With the exception of the bread before it is fried, every single ingredient on this list was going to be hard to come by during the war. Twelve rashers of bacon would

constitute about four people's weekly ration; the butter and the fat to fry the bread another person's weekly ration; lemons turned up occasionally if you happened to be in the right place at the right time; tomatoes you could grow yourself, but you would struggle to buy them, and bananas were simply not available.

PINEAPPLE CANDLESTICKS

bananas
pineapple slices
glacé cherries
candied angelica

1 Allow 1 banana for each slice of pineapple. Cut a slice off each banana and stand it in the hole of the pineapple. Put a stoned cherry on top of each banana to represent a flame, and fix a handle of angelica on each pineapple slice.

Apart from the eye-watering nature of the presentation, this is simply a fruit salad and absolutely none of the ingredients could be obtained during wartime if you lived on a farm in the country.

4oz bacon and ham

12oz sugar

2oz tea

1oz cheese

2oz preserves

2oz cooking fat

4oz butter

Meat was allocated by price – initiall.y you could buy meat up to a value of 1/10d.

THE FOOD RATION

Rationing is a confusing word, linked in many people's minds with the doling out of food rations to service personnel. But the wartime rationing system was nothing to do with supplying food to people, but rather placing a limit on how much they were allowed to buy.

Bacon, ham, butter and sugar were the first foodstuffs to be rationed, in January 1940, with meat following two months later, then tea and margarine in July, and cheese joining the system at the beginning of 1941. But rationing was not a static thing in the war – the amount a person could buy was carefully moderated according to the national food supply. The sugar ration, for example, was 1lb per person at one point and only 8oz at another. The safe arrival of a convoy, or a storage difficulty, could lead to a rise in the ration, just as losses at sea, a more pressing need for non-foodstuffs, or bombed-out docks and warehouses could see the ration drop.

If you lay one person's weekly ration out on a table, you can see that there really isn't much there at all. Just 1oz of cheese is particularly meagre-looking. My own grandfather came home on his first leave and ate the entire weekly cheese ration in one sandwich, to the silent horror of of my mother. The next day he asked for another cheese sandwich for tea and my grandmother had to explain that he had eaten the lot. He was mortified. Servicemen had separate catering arrangements and he had had no idea how small the civilian ration was.

For those in charge of feeding the family, it was the scarcity of fats that pinched most. Pastry is one-third fat, cake is a quarter fat, you need fat for frying, fat to brown meat, and vegetables for making stews and casseroles, as well as butter or marg for all those sandwiches.

PRICE OR POINTS

The money-based method of meat rationing was helpful, allowing you to choose between small amounts of good-quality expensive cuts and larger volumes of cheaper cuts, depending on your particular need or wish. It helped the national supply by increasing demand for all the normally less popular bits, such as lungs, ears and trotters, and it allowed the more adventurous cooks a little room for manoeuvre.

As the war continued, a whole range of other foodstuffs began to be in short supply, and a second system to try to ensure fairness of access to what there was in stock was introduced alongside the basic ration. It began with tinned meat and fish and beans but soon covered biscuits, dried fruit, dried pulses, and a host of other things. There were simply not enough of any of these goods to go around the whole population, but the points system allowed people to have a selection of what was available. Each food type was "priced" at a certain number of points, and individuals were allocated a number of points to spend. You could save up your points for as long as you liked, and could use them to buy anything that you could find in the shops. This was where being a townie on the spot when supplies arrived really made a difference. Many a country woman could only sigh, rather later in the day, at the empty shelves and her fistful of points coupons.

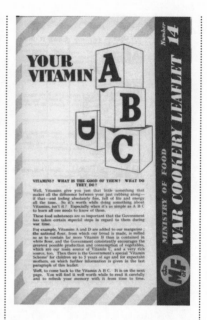

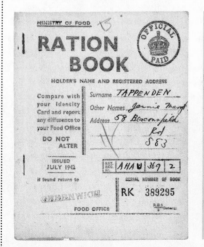

Above: Rationing was intended to provide a healthy diet, not just an adequate one. Leaflets such as this sought to help people make good food choices.

Far left: Ration books were intended to ensure a fair share for all.

Left: Tea rationing is something that I, as a tea addict, find particularly hard. How about a swap – my sugar ration for your tea ration?

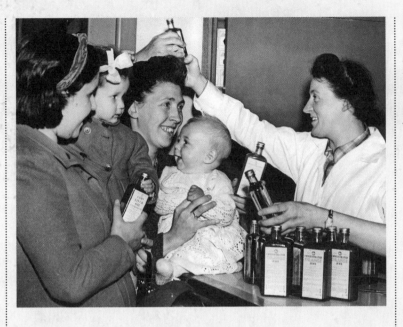

THE EFFECT OF RATIONING ON HEALTH

War work and rationing between them made a huge impact upon the health of the nation. The all too common smattering of emaciated children, encountered with horror by the families they were evacuated to at the start of the war, looked in general a lot sturdier by its end. For many of the planners of rationing, this had been a major goal all along. The pre-war subcommittee on rationing had been led by Sir William Beveridge. He and many of his staff saw rationing as a way of tackling the serious hunger-induced health issues of the day. Pre-war politics had stifled the efforts of many reformers to tackle public health issues; in rationing, they saw their chance. The rationed diet was not intended to be just for barest survival, but for healthy life. Fats, proteins, carbohydrates, vitamins and minerals were all incorporated into the rationing scheme.

Health supplements were targeted at the most vulnerable. National dairy production was to be reserved for expectant mothers and small children, regardless of their wealth or status. Only when this group had received what they needed was any surplus directed at the general population. Concentrated orange juice, with its high vitamin C content, was also targeted at this group. Expectant mothers could also get extra meat, and cod liver oil was constantly being pushed for children. It all made a difference. In raw statistical terms, the infant mortality rate in England and Wales in 1939 was 59 per 1,000, in 1944 it had fallen to 46 per 1,000. That's a lot fewer dead babies. Mothers' health was also markedly improving, as fewer died in childbirth. But whilst these figures show something of the improvement at the margins of life, they fail to highlight the improvements in most people's general health and fitness, which are less easy to quantify. Most people who lived through the war agree "we were healthier then". Not a very scientific statement, but an indication of how people perceived the health of those around them. The wealthy and middle classes might well have felt the benefits of more exercise and perhaps a better balanced diet, but it was the poorer people who really gained from rationing. Many of those who had suffered through the great depression ate better during the war than they had ever eaten in their lives. It wasn't that rationed food was particularly tasty, abundant or wonderful, but they were getting more of it.

Above: Cod liver oil was part of a concerted attempt to improve the diet and health of the nation's children.

THE GREY & BLACK MARKET
THE CURRENCY OF THE EGG

» ALEX LANGLANDS

It is a well-known fact that those in the countryside didn't feel the pinch of rationing quite so hard as those in the towns. Although many in suburbia turned their ornamental gardens over to small vegetable patches and reared a few chickens or rabbits, for the most part access to food in the cities was restricted to the rationing system. In the country, however, the opportunities for illicitly acquiring food beyond the ration quota were many and varied. In an economy that had little access to cash, a whole host of items would be employed in the bartering and exchange of desired goods. Food was high on this list, and a "black market" economy developed wherein one particular type of food was to emerge as a form of hard currency: the humble egg. In a diet potentially short on protein, eggs were seen as a luxury, both on taste and health grounds. In fact, eggs were considered so healthy that the government took the decision in June 1941 to subsidize retail egg prices. The objective of this scheme was to keep the general cost of living down, and egg producers with more than 50 birds were legally obliged to send all their eggs to packing stations in return for a price that outstripped what they could get by going direct to retail. Despite this offer of raised prices, many farmers kept their eggs back, feeling they could still use eggs more effectively in what was becoming a flourishing black market.

TRADE IN LUXURIES

This trade in food outside the pale of the government-sanctioned rationing system operated on a number of levels and to varying degrees of illegality. On the one hand, luxuries that had become extremely scarce in wartime Britain could, in some cases, only be acquired on the black market, and eggs were very well placed to use as a trade-off against things like cigarettes, gin, butter or dried exotic fruits. Thus, food that would otherwise have found its way into the rationing system, serving the greater good as part of the war effort, was being selfishly hived off for private enjoyment. However, eggs were also used to barter with neighbours who perhaps had a more productive vegetable patch. In this second instance, it is difficult to identify the level of exchange as being entirely "black market" and, in reality, what emerged was a kind of "grey market" where the distinction between criminality and mutual support became blurred. What, after all, was the real harm in exchanging a couple of eggs for a handful of leeks?

Increased mobility and interconnectivity between town and country meant that opportunities for exchange opened up. Those with access to the countryside through the use of a motorcar could head out for a morning's drive in pursuit of the much sought-after luxury of eggs. Hoteliers, in particular,

under pressure to impress their clientele, would loiter at the farm gate with tempting offers of cash or ration vouchers. Young men billeted in a rural setting or girls in service on the land found that eggs were easier to come by in the countryside than they had been in the cities, where their relatives still resided. Out of this, a healthy shuttle service of egg boxes was to develop. We read of one ingenious chap who had devised a wooden box divided into twelve compartments that he lined with felt. The eggs, before being placed into these compartments, would be wrapped individually in greaseproof paper so that if one was to break it could still be poured from the paper and used.

In the country, the opportunities for illicitly acquiring food beyond the ration quota were many and varied.

On our farm, decisions had been made to lose some of the poultry breeds reared mainly for their meat value because of the scarcity of feedstuffs. But I felt, for the most part, that Manor Farm's chickens were a wily bunch and good forage chickens that could look after themselves pretty well from the grubs, seeds and berries that can be found naturally in and around a farm. We were therefore in a perfect position to exploit the black

market hunger for eggs, and Peter and I opted to send some of our precious eggs in the post. After scratching our heads for a while in consideration of which of our city-based relatives would be most grateful for a dozen of our farm eggs, we decided instead to send them back to ourselves, in a bid to see if the modern postal service could take as much care and attention as that used so effectively by the illicit egg dealers of the early 1940s!

HOME FOOD PRODUCTION

» RUTH GOODMAN

FORAGING

The countryside offered those with access and the know-how an additional source of food throughout the war. In spring, there were a range of edible salad leaves, buds, and shoots that could be gathered from hedgerows. Dandelion leaves are a good tangy salad ingredient if you pick them early in the year when they are young and lush. Young nettle tops make a good spinach alternative and very tasty soup. Primrose flowers are truly delicious, but make sure that you only eat the petals and not the green parts of the plant. (Primroses are now protected so it is illegal to pick them in the wild.) Hawthorn buds have long been nibbled on by country people, and the young vigorous shoots of the elder tree can be peeled and eaten like celery.

SUMMER BOUNTY

In summer, fruits began to appear for those who knew where to look, beginning with wild strawberries and woodland raspberries. In autumn, the variety and quantities of fruit increase markedly – plums, damsons and apples can provide huge gluts, with nuts and mushrooms joining the list. Pigeons and rabbits were fair game if you could catch them; indeed ,the farmers would be pleased if you did, as they could do a deal of harm to crops. This was all traditional knowledge that long-term country dwellers knew, but now a host of evacuated townies were picking up tips as well as the odd mouthful. But we must remember how much time it takes to gather these free harvests, set against how much actual food you end up with. Some are more worth the bother than others. Yes, you can gather hawthorn hips, but the effort involved in turning a large bag of them into a small pot of something edible is considerable. If you live near a hazel copse, then a nutting trip is well worthwhile, particularly as hazelnuts keep so well, but is it worth an hour's walk in each direction?

In general, it was children who went foraging during the war. They had more time on their hands than the hard-pressed adults and as they were not engaged in other paid work, anything they brought home was additional not alternative. Like so many wartime country-dwelling children, my father's memories of wartime are full of foraging expeditions. Brought up in a small market town, he and his brother were encouraged to get out from beneath their mother's feet. Roaming the fields and lanes unsupervised, they picked their way through many different types of wild harvest, some for the family to eat and some to sell. What they brought home was rarely enough to make a meal as such, but handfuls of this and that could enliven a fairly boring wartime diet no end. Plain suet pudding is bland and dull, but add a good helping of blackberries and you have a much more appetising meal for no extra cost and no extra coupons.

Wild harvests were rarely enough to make a meal, but they could enliven a boring wartime diet.

ELDERFLOWER CORDIAL

You can make a quick cordial by adding a spoonful of sugar and boiling water to a handful of elderflower florets and then straining them, but here is a recipe that would also have been achievable in wartime if you had saved your sugar ration. Most recipes add tartaric or ascorbic acid or lemons to provide acidity. However, as long as you don't keep the cordial for more than a week (in the fridge), you don't need these – very useful in wartime, as lemons were scarce. For the best results, make your cordial as quickly as possible after gathering the flowers.

Makes 2 pints

| 50 freshly picked elderflower heads |
| 2½ pints of boiling water |
| 2½lb white sugar |

1 Pick your elderflowers on a sunny morning, as the perfume and starch content will be higher and your cordial will be sweeter.

2 Shake the flowers gently to make sure that there are no bugs.

3 Put the flowers and sugar in an enamel or a glass bowl. Pour over the boiling water until immersed.

4 Cover and leave to steep for 24 hours in a cool place.

5 Strain through a muslin cloth and discard the florets.

6 Bring gently to the boil, stirring.

7 Take off the heat, cool until tepid, pour into sterilized bottles and seal. As long as your solution is at least 60 per cent sugar, your cordial won't ferment.

PIG CLUBS

In 1944, there were 2,500,000 fewer pigs in Britain than there had been in 1939. This, of course, was no accident. What feed there was for livestock was carefully targeted where it could do most good, and although pigs grow fast and provide good eating, the acreage required to grow enough food to raise a pig can be used to grow more food for people. Grain and potatoes feed more people per acre than meat of any sort. So after much deliberation, both at the ministry and on each farm, hard decisions were taken: which animals to keep and which to send to slaughter. Cattle were the most likely livestock to be kept, especially dairy cows. Meanwhile, poultry, sheep and pig numbers fell rapidly and substantially.

Pig clubs were one way in which this decline in meat production was mitigated. If farmers didn't have enough feed, then the wider population could step in to bridge at least some of the gap with pigswill from their kitchens and gardens. We found ourselves in exactly this situation. When we took over the farm, it was a mixed concern, with beef and dairy cattle, some sheep, a dozen breeding sows and a scattering of poultry.

The sheep were the first to go, the beef cattle not far behind. Nor did the pigs seem like a good use of our resources, and the boys thought that they should all go. We agreed that there was no spare feed for them, but I thought that we could manage something if we were to set up a pig club. We wouldn't be able to keep them all of, course, but maybe one breeding sow and one of her piglets.

Pre-war pigs, for the most part, lived in concrete floored pigsties, just as ours did. They took up little land and could be easily cleaned out. Unable to forage about, the pigs needed all their food to be found for them. Manufactured, nutritionally balanced pig feeds provided a simple way of providing everything a pig needed to grow as fast and efficiently as possible. A range of fodder crops were used to make the commercial pig feeds and were also fed directly to supplement them. But just as commercial manufactured feed was in short supply during the war, acreage for fodder crops was under enormous pressure. If we were to keep pigs without feed, we would also have to do it without fodder.

An older way of keeping pigs had been to feed them on kitchen and garden waste. Indeed, on a small scale many people still did this. But it takes a lot of kitchen and garden waste to feed a pig, and wartime kitchens couldn't afford to waste very much. Many villagers in the past had solved this problem by clubbing together to keep a pig. Several families pooled their money to buy a piglet, worked out a system of dividing up the labour involved, and then all supplied scraps to feed. Everyone then shared in the meat when it was slaughtered in the agreed proportions. It seemed an obvious answer. Here was a way that meat could be reared without taking food out of the mouths of people.

REGULATIONS AND RATIONS

The Small Pig Keeping Council in 1939 set about encouraging more people than ever to set up pig clubs, both in the towns and in the countryside. Small amounts of pig meal could be purchased to help with the enterprise. It was a huge success. A little too successful in some ways, as the pig clubs were soon consuming most of the available pig meal. In 1942, the ministry had to tighten up the regulations. If you slaughtered a pig, you either had to give up one person's bacon ration for the entire year or, if a pig was owned by several different families, you had to give up half the carcass to the ministry.

Another tightening up of the regulations came about after an outbreak of foot-and-mouth disease. To begin with kitchen and garden waste was collected by the pig clubs and cooked up into swill as and when they saw fit. But the outbreak showed that this could not be allowed to go on unchecked. If disease was to be avoided then the waste needed to be very thoroughly cooked at a high temperature to ensure that it was sterilized properly. Swill now had to be prepared at licensed premises.

OUR CLUB

Having asked around the neighbourhood and stuck up a series of posters, we finally got a steady trickle of people who said that they would be interested in setting up a pig club with us. We knew that we couldn't run our club exactly as it was run during the war, as the dreaded foot-and-mouth disease has once again reared its ugly head and led to a further tightening of the regulations. Since the 2001 outbreak – traced back to infected pigswill – pigs are no longer allowed to be fed on any food that has passed through a kitchen in any way, not upon vegetables grown on land that has had animal manure on it during the previous 60 days. These are quite stringent rules and quite different from those in force during the war. But none the less, a pig club was still possible so long as we fed our pigs not upon kitchen waste but upon garden waste.

FINDING FOOD

Our members seemed enthusiastic; they all had gardens or allotments that regularly produced food fit for pigs. Cabbage stalks, the leaves of parsnip plants, beetroot thinnings, carrots that have been attacked by wire worms, potatoes assaulted by slugs, pea stalks and pods and other odds and ends that a pig thinks are delicious. Windfall apples and pears were very gratefully received, and anything in storage that began to turn, such as carrots, potatoes or apples.

Another potential source of pig food was the countryside around us. Way back in the Middle Ages, when pigs had been driven into the woods to forage, they had fattened nicely on a diet of beetles, grubs, roots and, especially, acorns. We were surrounded by good hedgerows and woodland at Manor Farm. Acorns, beechnuts and chestnuts are high

Top: From our four piglets, we decided to keep the piglet that was the keenest on our pigswill.
Above: Windfalls are useful pig food.
Left: Our piglet, Shorty, is second from the left.
Right: Our breeding sow is not the most beautiful of pigs, but she had a wonderful personality! Those who were sent to market were prettier, but grumpier.

in fats and proteins and made a really nutritious addition to our garden waste. The official advice for acorns was to collect, dry, peel, and grind them before adding to the pigswill. This proved to be a fiddly and time-consuming operation, but it wasn't unpleasant work. Having prepared my first (and probably only) large sack full of acorns, our first meeting of the pig club got underway. I lit up the old copper in the wash house and brought a bucket full of water up to the boil along with the parsley roots that I had just dug up from the garden. Gill, Gill, and Terry were our first members to arrive, each with a full bucket. Gill the First remembered her own parents belonging to a pig club during the war, so I felt that she was going to be a very useful member. Gill the Second and Terry were both keen gardeners, too, so we would hopefully have plenty of swill to keep our pigs going.

With a bucket of pigswill in hand, I went down to the yard to choose our pig. Snowflake, the Middle White sow, had a small but healthy litter of four. The female with the short tail seemed keener than the rest on the unfamiliar pisgswill, so Shorty it was. Snowflake would stay to produce new litters. We would try to persuade other pig clubs to take on the rest of the litter, but our other pigs would have to go to slaughter.

PRESERVING THE MEAT

» PETER GINN

During the war, there were around 6,900 pig clubs with approximately 100,000 members all feeding their animals on their kitchen scraps, ensuring nothing went to waste. However, when you send your 85 kg porcine pal to the big farm in the sky that leaves you with a lot of meat to consume, but there are a number of ways to cure the meat and preserve it for a meal at a later date.

My favourite way of preserving leftover pork is to pot it. I tend to slow-cook pork in a mix of anything to hand, including, but not limited to, honey, cloves, garlic, Coca-Cola (keeps the meat very tender) and cider. The resulting meat is very moist and friable but I always find there is too much. I cram the leftovers into pots and cover with a layer of fat (usually butter, as I like to have these pots as a lunch with toast, but during the war, when butter was scarce, the pots would have been sealed using fat rendered from the pork) to keep the air out. This form of preservation gave way to canning, which is essentially the same process but using a tin as a seal rather than the fat of the pig.

SALTING AND DRYING

The other usual way of preserving pork is to desiccate it, primarily through salting to draw the moisture out. It is a simple process of rubbing large quantities of salt on the cut of pork, placing weights on top and later draining the liquid before reapplying the salt and the weight over a period of days (this depends on the size of the cut). During the salting process, spices can be added for flavour, and sugar is often added to counteract the bitterness of the salt. After salting, the meat can be cold smoked (at a temperature below 37°C), adding an antibacterial layer to the meat. The smoking process uses wood chips from trees such as oak, alder or apple. Alternatively, it can be hung up to air dry for a period of several months.

One final and easy method of curing pork is to pickle it. There are a number of ways to do this but the simplest is to bring to the boil a mix of vinegar, sugar, and spices, let this cool, then add your cured pork and seal it in a container. It is rewarding to think that you are curing your own meat and fun to do. However, one must always be aware of the parasites that can occur in semi-cured meats, such as trichinosis, and that some cured meats such as green bacon must be cooked prior to eating.

Above: A piece of boneless pork belly in the process of being salted.

HONEY-CURED BACON

Makes about 4lb

1lb 2oz coarse sea salt

3 bay leaves, chopped

15 juniper berries, crushed

4lb 4oz thick piece of boned pork belly, rind left on

14oz honey

1 Put the salt, bay leaves and juniper berries into a mortar and crush until you have a coarse mixture. Put the pork on a scrupulously clean kitchen worktop or chopping board and rub about ⅔ of the cure into it.

2 Put the pork into a non-reactive container (something plastic is good) and pour ⅔ of the honey on the top flesh side of the bacon and rub it in. Cover. Put the pork in the fridge or somewhere very cold (it needs to be about 5°C).

3 Reserve the rest of the cure and the honey. After a day, you'll see liquid has gathered around the pork. Pour off this liquid and rub the pork with more cure and pour on more honey. Repeat the following day, using all the remaining cure and honey. Keep in the cold place for another 2 days, so it has 5 days curing altogether. The pork should feel firm and is now bacon.

4 Rinse off the excess cure in warm water and dry the pork. Wrap it in muslin or cheesecloth and keep in the fridge or hang it up somewhere just as cold. The bacon will dry out and develop flavour over the next couple of days. Just cut pieces off – either thick rashers or chunks – as you need them. It will keep for 2 weeks.

POTTED PORK

Makes 14oz

1lb cooked pork belly, at room temperature

5 tablespoons duck or goose fat, plus extra to top the pots

3 large shallots or ½ onion, finely chopped

12 sage leaves

4 sprigs thyme, leaves chopped

2 teaspoons mixed spice

really generous grating of nutmeg

salt and black pepper

1 Chop the cooked pork belly, together with its fat (though not the crackling) as finely as you can – you really need to mince it. If you have a mincer, you can put it through that.

2 Melt a little of the poultry fat in a pan and gently sauté the onion or shallot until soft but not coloured. Put this in a bowl with the minced pork and all the other ingredients and pound together with a pestle. You want to end up with a coarse, pâté-like texture. If it seems a little dry, add more duck or goose fat. Season well and be generous with the spicing – essential for good potted meats.

3 Put the mixture into sterilized pots or jars, leaving about ½ inch at the top. Spoon on enough melted fat to cover the meat (lard actually makes a good seal: use one that is denser than duck or goose fat, if you have that to hand) and seal. Keep in the fridge or somewhere really cold such as a cellar.

PRESERVING

» RUTH GOODMAN

The bounty of the countryside would have been of little use to anyone if it had gone unpreserved. Whilst the stalwart members of the Women's Institute were doing their best to preserve as much as possible for the nation (see pages 128–31), a countrywoman still needed to preserve her own personal supplies. The produce of the hard-working preservation centres went into the general food chain. Despite their labour and the fruit they supplied, the women themselves got none of the produce.

STORING FRUIT

Apples were in particular abundance on Manor Farm, but there is only so much jam a family can eat – always supposing that they could get hold of enough sugar to make large quantities of jam. What was really wanted was a series of sugarless preservation methods.

The simplest, and in many ways the most useful, is cool storage. Applelofts are cool, dark, dry places where the apples can sit out the winter by themselves, gently getting a bit wrinkly and a lot sweeter. Some varieties keep better than others, but in essence any unblemished apple can be stored for many weeks and months so long as it is dry and untouched by any other rotting apple. As a general rule, the later a variety of apple ripens in the year, the better its keeping qualities. Eaters keep better than cookers usually and, for some reason, green-coloured varieties are less long-lasting than red-coloured fruit, although there are exceptions. The great walled gardens of the aristocracy had long had special apple storage buildings as part of their overall infrastructure, but you don't need a specially built place to store apples. The key criteria were that an area had to be dry, unheated and airy. Garden sheds were perfect. The apples need to be laid out gently so that no two apples

touch in any direction. A series of trays lined with newspaper or straw was ideal. If the trays are slatted and the newspaper shredded, it is even better, as that allows free flow of air around the fruit and prevents condensation collecting. A piece of dry sacking over the top to cut down the light is helpful, too. Once laid out in their trays, the apples would need to be checked over every couple of weeks. If any began to rot, they would need to be removed immediately before the moulds and rot spread. A good apple loft stocked with a keeping variety could yield edible fruit six months after the apples first went into store.

DRYING APPLES

Even longer-lasting than apple loft apples were dried apples. This requires a good deal more work, but no more ingredients. Again, the fruit needed to be unblemished. There was absolutely no point in trying to preserve blemished fruit, as they would be already compromised – the bacteria- and mould-resistant seal (known as the skin) – would have been breached.

BLACKBERRY AND APPLE LEATHER

Makes 2 sheets

| 10oz blackberries |
| 1½lb cooking apples, peeled, cored and chopped |
| 5 tablespoons runny honey |

1 Preheat the oven to its lowest setting – the warmth of an Aga is perfect.

2 Put the blackberries and apples in a pan and cook gently over a low heat for about 15–20 minutes, or until soft.

3 Take off the heat and push through a sieve into a bowl, then stir in the honey.

4 Spread out thickly onto two baking sheets lined with oiled greaseproof paper, about ¼ inch thick.

5 Bake for 12–15 hours, or until it is dry and peels off the paper. Leave to cool, then roll it up on its paper and store in an airtight container in a cool place. Use within three months.

DRIED APPLE ROUNDS

Makes about 40 rounds

| 6 apples, peeled and sliced into rounds |
| 2 pints water |
| 1 tablespoon coarse salt |

1 Mix the water and salt in a large basin and drop in the apples to stop them from browning. Many commercially dried apples have their cores removed at this stage leaving apple rings rather than rounds, but for home production I recommend leaving the core in, as it provides strength and cohesion during the drying process.

2 Drain the apple rounds but do not rinse, and pat dry with a clean cloth. Thread the rounds onto string or skewers and hang up to dry. Then comes the technical bit. The atmosphere they are hung up in is very important – dry and warm with a good airflow is what you are after. Greenhouses are great if you keep the doors and ventilators open. In our cottage, I found the area halfway up the stairs with its south-facing window was perfect.

3 After about a week when the fruit is reasonably dry and feels a bit spongy and springy, it can be packed up in paper bags to continue drying for a few weeks before finally being sealed up in tins or jars.

JAM – THE NATION'S FAVOURITE

Jam was a staple food in pre-war Britain, and remained so throughout the war. It may seem an odd foodstuff to single out, but it had a significance way beyond its modern role. In the 19th century, sugar had become a cheap commodity. So cheap, in fact, that it became a working class staple. The energy that can be obtained from small amounts of sugar is great; it moves quickly into the bloodstream, giving a very noticeable lift. Cheap sugar had led to cheap jam, much cheaper than dripping. The working classes of Britain had long survived largely on bread, and a smear of jam made it both more palatable and significantly raised its calorific content. At the outbreak of World War II, bread and jam, also known as "a piece", was still the cheapest meal available and one that many city dwellers, in particular, regularly had to make do with. A farmer may have been lucky enough to have a wedge of cheese or a slice of ham in his lunchtime sandwiches, but if money was tight, then it was back to jam.

REDUCING THE SUGAR

With nearly three-quarters of our sugar being imported at the outbreak of war, it was apparent that sugar and jam, so cheap and so relied on, would be in short supply. Sugar was one of the first foodstuffs to be rationed. Finding ways of making jam with less sugar therefore became something of a priority. Ambrose Heath, the presenter of the radio programme *The Kitchen Front*, devoted a fair number of broadcasts to the subject of low-sugar jams. The recipes and hints he gave out over the air were also published in book form to help the housewife with fruit collected from the garden. His recommended aids are salt, glucose syrup and saccharin, all of which could cut down, if not entirely replace, the sugar required.

Salt was used to halve the quantity of sugar. The proportions are: for 4lb of fruit, use 2lb of sugar, and one to two teaspoonfuls of salt. As he points out, this recipe doesn't keep as long as one using 4lb of sugar to match the 4lb of fruit, and doesn't taste quite so sweet. He claims, however, that the salt helps to bring out the flavour of the fruit. In both of these observations, he is absolutely correct. The better-quality modern jam producers use these proportions on a regular basis. It is generally cheaper brands that use the equal proportion of fruit to sugar, as sugar is currently very much cheaper than fruit.

Glucose syrup was less successful. It would only replace one quarter of the sugar, and could itself be difficult to get hold of, although it makes perfectly nice jam if you do. Saccharin was a common wartime replacement for sugar in many different foodstuffs. Three-quarters of the sugar could be replaced with saccharin, but you would have to use gelatine to actually set the jam.

PRESERVED FRUIT

Makes 4 jars

4lb cooked fruit
1lb sugar
40 saccharin tablets
4 packets of gelatine, sufficient to set 4 pints of liquid

1 Stir the sugar into the cooked fruit pulp, dissolve the saccharin tablets and the gelatine in a little hot water and stir thoroughly into the sweetened fruit. Pour into sterilised jars and allow to set.

This recipe doesn't taste that great in truth, but if needs must...

Above: Bread and jam was a staple food for wartime workers.

CANNING WITH THE WOMEN'S INSTITUTE
CALLING IN THE EXPERTS

» RUTH GOODMAN

When we moved into Manor Farm, autumnal fruitfulness surrounded us. Exactly as had happened in 1939, the autumn was long, golden and warm. The plums and greengages had just about all fallen but the apple trees were laden with a bumper crop. No matter how hard I tried, there was simply too much fruit for one woman to preserve. This was a common experience in the countryside of 1939, and with everyone aware that war was going to mean food shortages, it seemed a terrible waste. Luckily, some thought had already been put into the problem, most practically by the Women's Institute, or WI.

Originally a Canadian idea, the WI in England was set up during World War I as an organization of countrywomen. Indeed, town-dwelling women were unable to join until the 1960s. Its purposes were several – to provide mutual support for women in the countryside and to help mobilize their talents and efforts. From

Among a host of other areas of responsibility, the WI also took on the preservation of fruit that would otherwise have gone to waste.

the first, it was a campaigning organization, promoting women's issues, raising women's self-esteem and raising awareness more generally of the skills, work and contribution of countrywomen. But it was also a practical organization, involved right from its inception in essential war work and in training women.

With World War II on the horizon, it is perhaps not all that surprising that this organization, set up in wartime, tried, tested and proven in its organizational skills, should be called upon again by the government for help. In some ways, the WI and, later, the Women's Voluntary Service were to be used almost as minor government departments. It was the WI, for example, that

Far left: Seasonal gluts of fruit could easily have gone to waste if the WI had not stepped in.

Left: WI preservation centres were run as small factory concerns, with local women providing free fruit and free labour. Here, Ruth is being given valuable WI advice by historian Anne Stamper.

organised and supervised the whole evacuation effort, and that ran billeting systems throughout the war, all on a voluntary basis and with little government or military assistance.

PRESERVING

Among a host of other areas of responsibility, the WI also took on the preservation of fruit that would otherwise have gone to waste. It was in this guise that

I was to first encounter the wartime WI. The WI and jam go together like bacon and eggs in most of our minds, and so they should. The volume of additional food entering the national food supply was substantial, and came in several forms – a lot of jam and jelly, but also plenty of chutney, bottled fruit and canned fruit.

With so many surplus apples, I was keen to see how this preservation scheme worked

in practice. The first thing that struck me was how ordered and professional the whole set-up was. It may well have been undertaken by volunteer women in village halls, but don't be deceived into thinking that that meant slapdash or insignificant. In effect, these preserving centres functioned as a series of small factories. Every gift of fruit was weighed and logged, records were kept of how much sugar was used in each batch, and each batch was weighed and recorded. Sugar was, of course, in short supply, and every grain had to be accounted for. The Ministry of Food allowed WI preserving centres a supply outside of the members' personal rations to preserve the fruit, but obviously they expected very rigorous control. The amount of sugar was carefully calculated for each recipe to provide the best keeping qualities with the least sugar. This made canning a good option. Canned fruit requires much less sugar than jam or jelly to keep it edible, and much less than bottled fruit in general.

Sealing the cans required use of a small canning device. This piece of equipment was something that many WIs had to raise money to buy. Whilst most of the other equipment was cobbled together from members' own households, the machines were really too expensive for individuals to justify buying privately before the war, so there were few about. Some WIs were lucky enough to receive one of the machines donated by Canadian WI members to help their English counterparts in the war effort. Most, however, held a series of jumble sales and whist drives to finance the purchase.

Daily totals of production and records of where it went, whether to local schools and canteens or into the more general supply chain were kept. The women worked full shifts in teams, keeping the centre running usually two days a week for the next five years. Remember, these were unpaid volunteers who had farms and families to run as well. Small village centres like ours were generally turning out around 32kg (70lb) weight of finished product a day, using free fruit that would otherwise have simply rotted.

CANNING THE FRUIT

I have jammed, jellied, bottled and chutneyed with the best of them, but I had never canned anything before. In truth, I was rather surprised to discover that domestic-sized canning kits were available, I had always assumed that you needed large factory-scale equipment. It turned out, however, to be relatively straightforward, so long as you were scrupulously careful to maintain good hygiene at every stage. Imperfectly canned goods can be dangerous in two ways. The most common problem is "blowing". When the can is improperly prepared and sealed, decay or fermentation inside can cause a build-up of gas, which can lead the can to explode. The other danger is eating the contents of an improperly prepared can; bacteria can breed, causing some nasty food poisoning – occasionally fatal.

Aware of these dangers, the WI had a strict training regime to drum into people the importance of accuracy, particularly in the sterilizing procedures.

Left: Accurate and thorough sterilization was essential.
Right above: The canning machine was simplicity itself to use.
Right: Apples were packed as tightly as possible into the cans.

CANNED APPLES

apples
salt
sugar

1 Pick over the fruit, discarding anything bruised, pitted or worm-eaten.

2 Wipe, weigh, peel and core the fruit, then immediately put into a bowl of salted water to stop them from browning.

3 Meanwhile, prepare the sugar syrup: mix together the sugar and water in a saucepan and bring to the boil.

4 Pack the prepared fruit into cans taking care to get as much fruit as possible into each one. Pour the boiling syrup over the fruit in the can ¼in from the top, then place a lid on top.

5 Use the canning machine: 20 turns of the handle seals one can. Mind you, it has to be exactly 20 turns of the handle, neither more nor less, and you must start with it in the right position – it becomes quick and easy once you get into the swing of it.

6 Next comes the critical bit – sterilizing the contents of the newly sealed can. Submerge the can "up to its neck" in water, bringing that water slowly up to the boil and simmering for exactly 18 minutes to kill any bacteria inside the can. Once sterilized, leave to cool. Then label and pack.

Easy peasy. Just don't make a mistake!

WARTIME RECIPES

» RUTH GOODMAN

Most of us like to eat familiar food, especially in times of stress. Comfort food usually reminds us of our childhood, and exploring completely new foods is something that most of us see as an occasional adventure. Wartime Britons were no different, but wartime ingredients were often not as familiar as they would have liked. Haricot beans, for example, were new to many, but they were plentifully available from America, easy to transport and high in nutritional value. As well as new foods appearing, however, a lot of familiar foods were scarce or absent. Enter the substitutes. Ways of making the unfamiliar seem familiar, ways of creating some memory of favourite foods from what was still available were highly prized, and all sorts of recipes did the rounds to help people cope with the range of ingredients actually on offer.

SPRING SOUP

Watercress, endive or sorrel may be used, either with or in place of the lettuce for a change.

Serves 6

1 large lettuce
12 spring onions
dripping, for frying
1 pint stock or water
1 pint milk
1 tablespoon cornflour
sugar, to taste
nutmeg, to taste
salt and pepper
crusts of bread, for croutons
curly parsley, leaves picked and chopped

1 Wash the lettuce and onions, then shred the lettuce and slice the onions thinly.
2 Melt a spoonful of dripping in a saucepan and fry the lettuce and onions for about 5 minutes.
3 Add the stock and half the milk, and allow to simmer gently for 10 minutes.
4 Mix the cornflour with the remainder of the milk, then pour into the soup. Stir until it boils, allowing to simmer for another 10 minutes.
5 Season to taste with sugar, a little nutmeg and salt and pepper.
6 Cut the crusts of bread into

thin strips, dry in a low oven until quite crisp, put them into a tureen with the parsley and pour over the soup.

MOCK FISH

A recipe from Ambrose Heath's book *More Kitchen Front Recipes*.

Serves 2–3

½ pint milk, plus extra for brushing

2oz ground rice

1 teaspoon chopped onion or leek

a spoonful of margarine, the size of a walnut

anchovy essence, to season (optional)

1 egg, beaten

handful of breadcrumbs

Fish was pretty scarce during the war, with few fishermen still working at their old trade, many having been called into the navy, and many waters out of bounds to civilians. What fish there was was quickly snapped up by local coastal people, and little made its way inland to farmers like us. This recipe is quite a good one, definitely better than many vegetarian fish substitutes that I have had.

1 Pour the milk into a pan and bring it to the boil. Add the ground rice, chopped onion or leek, the margarine and the anchovy essence.

2 Let this simmer gently for 20 minutes, then take the pan off the stove, and stir in the beaten egg. Mix well together, then transfer to a flat dish and spread the mixture out, 7–8 inches in diameter.

3 Cut into pieces the size and shape of fish fillets, brush with milk and roll in breadcrumbs. Fry until golden brown. Serve with parsley sauce.

MOCK MARMALADE

This is one of my favourite wartime recipes, not so much for its flavour, which is pleasant but not wonderful, but for the wistful longing it creates. I have found several similar recipes, one in a booklet published by the WI, another in a copy of *Woman's Weekly*, a third in *Good Eating*. They all begin with an apple jelly, flavoured with some orange essence and filled with tiny shreds of carrot to mimic the peel. Crab apples are best for this if you can get them – they set well for a recipe that uses such a small amount of sugar and they have a bit of flavour of their own. I also find it worthwhile soaking the carrot shreds in the orange essence for an hour before adding both to the jelly just before you pot it up.

Makes 2 jars:

2 pints water
1lb crab apples
1 carrot
2 teaspoons orange essence
8oz sugar

1 Bring the water to the boil in a large pan. Chop up the apples, leaving the peel and cores in, and simmer gently in the water for about an hour with a lid firmly fixed on the pan.

2 Strain the juice through a tea towel or jelly bag into a clean pan, allowing it to drip through under the force of gravity only. If you squeeze it, the resultant marmalade will be cloudy. Don't be impatient – it is best to leave this to drip for a couple of hours. Meanwhile, peel and carefully craft your carrot 'orange peel' into whatever shapes you like and put them to soak in a small bowl with the orange essence.

3 Add your sugar to the strained apple juice and bring to a rolling boil. It will need to carry on boiling for about 20 minutes by which time it should begin to achieve a set, although the finished result will be a little runny. If you have a sugar thermometer, you are aiming for 104°C. If not, you should find that a drop of the juice when allowed to cool on a clean plate will set slightly and have a wrinkly skin when you lightly push a finger over the cold droplet. At this point, take the pan off the heat.

4 Skim the surface, then stir in the carrot shreds and the orange essence.

5 Pot up the mixture into sterilized jars. After potting, turn the jars from time to time so that the carrot shreds are evenly dispersed.

GINGERBREAD CAKE

Makes 1 cake

½lb self-raising flour
6oz golden syrup
2 teaspoons ground ginger
1 teaspoon bicarbonate of soda
¼ pint tepid water

1 Place the flour and syrup in a basin.

2 Mix the ginger and bicarbonate of soda with the tepid water, add to the flour and syrup, then mix together.

3 Turn into a greased tin about 11 x 7in, then bake in a moderate oven for about ¾–1 hour, or until firm to the touch.

4 Wrap in greaseproof paper and store in a tin. Do not cut for 2 days.

COCONUT ICE

Makes 30 squares

8oz sweetened condensed milk
8oz icing sugar, sifted, plus extra for dusting
7oz dessicated coconut
pink edible food colouring, optional

1 Mix together the condensed milk, icing sugar and dessicated coconut in a large bowl. It will get very stiff, so use your hands, if easier.

2 Divide the mixture in half and knead a very small amount of food colouring into one half.

3 Dust a board with icing sugar, then push the pink mixture into the base of a 2lb loaf tin lined with greaseproof paper. Press and smooth it into an even layer, then add the white layer and press this evenly on top until smooth. Leave to set – this will take approximately 1 hour.

4 Cut into squares with a sharp knife and pack into bags or boxes. This will keep for up to a month at least, provided it is stored in an airtight container.

All sorts of recipes did the rounds to help people cope with the range of ingredients actually on offer.

BAKED POTATO PUDDING

Serves 6

½lb potatoes

raspberry jam

1 teaspoon sugar

1 egg, beaten

juice of 1 swede (see page 231)

For the pastry:

6oz flour

½ teaspoon salt

½ teaspoon baking powder

¾oz fat

1 tablespoon golden syrup, warmed

1 Cook the potatoes in salted boiling water until tender. Drain, then cool.

2 To make the pastry, mix together the flour, salt and baking powder, then rub in the fat. Pour in the syrup and stir well to make a very stiff dough. Roll out while hot and use it to line a tin.

3 Spread the jam over the pastry.

4 Mash the potatoes, adding the sugar, beaten egg and a little of the swede juice. Spread the mixture over the jam and bake in a moderate oven.

MAKING SOFT CHEESE

Cheese is essentially separated milk. Almost like magic, when milk, a liquid, curdles, it becomes part-liquid and part-solid, the curds and whey of the little Miss Muffet nursery rhyme. When a young calf drinks its mother's milk, the enzymes in its stomach curdle the milk, kick-starting the process, and this is the very 'rennet' that we normally use in our own cheese making. Traditional cheese making has generally involved slaughtering one young calf from the herd at Easter time. Aside from eating the veal as the traditional Easter Sunday dinner, the calf's stomach was carefully preserved to provide cheese-making rennet for the rest of the year.

But although rennet makes the best cheese and produces the most from any given volume of milk, it is not the only way to curdle milk. Many acids will do the job for you, the most pleasant edible acids being lemon juice or a dash of vinegar. The juice of stinging nettles also has a long tradition as an active agent in traditional British cheese-making.

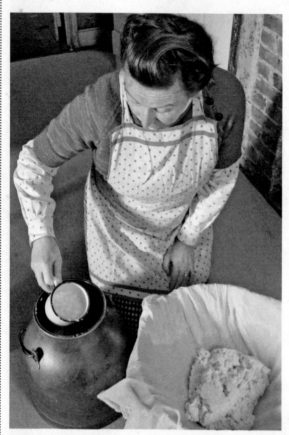

Above: Pouring the curdled milk through muslin means the whey drops into the container below and the curd is caught in the cloth, ready for cheese-making.

USING CURDLED MILK

If you leave milk long enough, however, it will "turn" all by itself, with a little help from naturally occurring bacteria. If you have ever had a bottle of milk go off, so that it is lumpy in the bottle, you have, in fact, made cheese. Pour that "off" milk through a fine strainer so that the liquid whey can run free, leaving you with the solid curd. And there you have it – you have produced perfectly good and edible cheese. A tiny sprinkle of salt will improve the flavour and also keep it sweet for your sandwich the next day.

With milking in full swing, there was always the possibility that we would find ourselves with a churn or two that wasn't picked up in time, with milk that was no longer saleable. This was ideal for some simple cheese making. Dairy farmers were allowed during the war to keep some of their own milk "for personal use" as a sort of bribe to encourage dairy production, so we could have taken a regular supply for home cheese-making if we had wanted to. But, along with most wartime dairy farmers, we had too many scruples and not enough spare time to do that. But the occasional churn of spoilt milk was a different matter. This would have otherwise just gone to waste and so we made ourselves some soft cheese. (This is not recommended for pregnant women and other vulnerable groups.)

1 A churn of milk that had curdled, or gone "off", yielded a whole mixing bowl of soft cheese for our sandwiches.

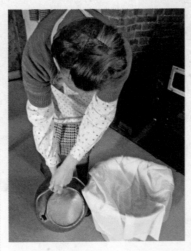

2 Lay a clean sieve over the top of a fresh clean container, then cover it with a large square of clean muslin. The important thing, as in all dairying, is strict hygiene. Everything you use must be scrupulously clean, preferably sterilized with boiling water.

3 Gently pour the churn of curdled milk through the cloth and sieve. The whey will drop through into the container below leaving the curd in the cloth on top. On a wartime farm, whey was excellent pig food, so it wouldn't go to waste.

4 Tie together the corners of the cloth and hang up somewhere cool to continue dripping overnight. Avoid overpressing, as the curd could break up into tiny gritty bits, which float away, losing much of the substance of your cheese.

5 In the morning, open up the cloth and gently break apart your cheese.

6 Sprinkle in a scattering of salt. A pint of milk would produce no more than an eggcup of curd and need only a tiny pinch of salt. My churn produced a serving bowl of curd, and I mixed in about half a teacup of salt.

EMERGENCY RESTAURANT FOR EVACUEES

» RUTH GOODMAN

With the ration set at equal levels for everyone, these British Restaurants could provide a calorific top-up for workers.

As bombs fell and people emerged from the shelters to find their homes obliterated, as new waves of workers arrived in an area, and as evacuee numbers rose and fell, the need to find some way of providing basic facilities became ever greater. Catering vans, which could turn up wherever and whenever they were needed, offering at the very minimum a cup of hot sweet tea, were the first line of defence.

EMERGENCY HELP

To cope with slightly longer-term arrangements, scout huts, church halls and other public buildings were pressed into service. Basic supplies could be bought off-ration and at subsidized rates by such centres to offer cheap but nutritious hot food to those who needed it urgently.

For the first 48 hours after a person had been bombed out, the meals were free, giving those who had nothing but the clothes on their backs a little breathing space and the reassurance they could at least eat while they made some basic arrangements.

Re-branded as British Restaurants, such establishments also had a more long-term role in feeding the workforce. People engaged in heavy physical labour burn more calories than those in sedentary occupations, and with the ration set at equal levels for everyone, these British Restaurants could provide a calorific top-up for workers. Their meals were off-ration and cheap: 2d would buy you a starter, 8d a main meal with potatoes and two veg, and 4d a pudding and a cup of tea.

SCHOOL DINNERS

My father remembers eating at such an establishment during the war. For six months, the British Restaurant in Hitchin provided his school dinners, dinners that included a lot of boiled onions in white sauce and carrots riddled with wireworm. They were hot, though, and filling. Once the kids had finished, the adults began to arrive, workers in the main, although there were also a scattering of the elderly for whom this represented the only sort of help on offer.

Looking at the list of supplies that one British Restaurant had in stock in 1942, I came up with a menu of boiled onions in white sauce, meat roll and gravy served with baked beans, mashed potatoes, and carrots (no wire worm, though), followed by plum duff and custard.

Right: The meat roll was not only extremely economical, but tasty, too.

BOILED ONIONS WITH WHITE SAUCE

Serves 8

2lb onions, left whole but peeled

1 pint milk (made from milk powder)

1oz cornflour

herbs from the garden, finely chopped

1 Boil the whole onions in water for 45 minutes, or until tender.

2 Meanwhile, make up milk according to the packet instructions. Heat gently, but do not boil.

3 Mix the cornflour with a little cold water until smooth. Pour into the milk and stir over a low heat until it thickens. Mix in whatever herbs you like. Serve with the onions.

MEAT ROLL

Serves 4

3oz breadcrumbs (made from stale bread)

¾lb sausage meat

5oz pinto beans, cooked and mashed

1 teaspoon powdered mustard

1 teaspoon thyme

gravy browning

browned breadcrumbs, to serve

salt and pepper

1 Soak the breadcrumbs in water until moist. Squeeze out the water and mash together with the sausage meat, the mashed beans, mustard, thyme and salt and pepper. Add enough gravy browning until it turns dark brown.

2 Wrap in damp, floured muslin, sew up the opening and steam for 2 hours.

3 Roll in brown breadcrumbs and serve hot with gravy.

PLUM DUFF

Use this method for steaming any savoury dish or pudding.

Serves 4

4oz plain flour

8oz raisins

4oz suet

4oz breadcrumbs

½ teaspoon mixed spice

2 eggs

8 fl oz milk

1 Combine the flour, raisins, suet, breadcrumbs and mixed spice.

2 Add the eggs and mix well.

3 Gradually add the milk until the mixture falls from the spoon when tapped on the side of the bowl.

4 Dampen a muslin cloth (3 foot square) and rub with flour inside and out, then drape the cloth over a large pudding basin.

5 Pour the mixture into the cloth and tie the ends together tightly. Leave a little room into which the cooking pudding can expand.

6 Steam for 45 minutes, topping up the water level in your pan.

CHAPTER FIVE
LIVESTOCK

Farming underwent a massive change to cope with the demands placed upon it by an island nation isolated by war. Livestock had been the salvation of many farmers during the troubled inter-war period, and by 1939 the majority of farms were a mix of animals and crops. However, the amount of land needed to rear an animal, versus the amount of calories that it would give to humans who consume it, is far less than the amount of calories that a crop grown on the same area of land would produce. This was why the government made the decision to make farmers turn large areas of grazing over to arable land.

This marked the end of the lives of many animals. Dairy cows were generally safe, but the production of mutton, lamb, beef and veal fell significantly. And it was definitely not a good time to be either a pig or a chicken, as both these animals were deemed not to give much back to the soil in return for what they ate. They were slaughtered en masse. Pig clubs and domestic poultry keepers did keep some of these animals alive, albeit largely away from farms.

LIFE ON THE FARM

» PETER GINN

Life on the farm entered a period of great change at the beginning of the war. Where once farms had largely comprised a mixture of arable (crops) and livestock, the Government's agricultural policies forced dramatic change. Convoys could no longer import the feed on which farmers had become reliant to feed their livestock during the pre-war years. It was with this in mind that the Government ordered the ploughing up of permanent pasture, to turn large areas of grazing over to arable land, sounding the death knell of much of Britain's livestock. It was during this period that many "rare breeds" became rare.

"ALL CHANGE"

Horse-power, although on the decline, saw a renewed role on the wartime farm. As kit was being dragged out of the hedgerows to be used on the farm, it was often the horses that did the dragging. We used horses to harrow our flax while we sowed the seed using a tractor. Without them we would never have managed to get the crop into the ground. Horses were also being used by the army to cross rough terrain in North Africa and the Mediterranean.

Beef cattle, although still being reared to feed the troops, declined in number, especially as dairy cattle were still very much in demand. Milk was a product that was desperately needed and it was something that we could produce in this country, but rearing a dairy herd must have represented a significant challenge when much of the land had been given over to arable, prompting farmers to make hay in unusual places, such as churchyards.

The same goes for sheep: numbers fell massively. Pig and chicken numbers also suffered, and rearing pigs became the preserve of pig clubs. During my childhood in Belgium, our school kept pigs, sustained entirely on the scraps from our lunches. During and after the war, similar waste was collected in bins dotted around street corners.

Chickens will survive on whatever they can forage, but the number that one can keep in this way is limited. However, the chicken's ability to find its own food encouraged many people to establish poultry clubs.

Pests such as rabbits and pigeons were shot and provided much needed meat. However, you had to be careful not to shoot a carrier pigeon. Out of the 54 recipients of the Dickin medal for animal bravery, 32 were awarded to pigeons.

At the start of the war, scared that they wouldn't have enough food to feed them, many people decided to destroy their pets. We, however, decided to keep Henry, the border collie (our ever-knowledgeable sound man's dog). Unlike other wartime dogs, Henry may not have been pressed into service finding bodies in rubble, but he provided us with much needed companionship and sometimes, that is what counts the most.

THE RETURN OF HORSEPOWER

» ALEX LANGLANDS

Below: Before the war, the majority of hard and heavy farm work was undertaken by heavy horses such as these two Clydesdale horses ploughing land in Mid-Lothian, Scotland, 1936.
Right: Robert Sampson drives Iona (dark grey) and Crystal (light-grey) pulling a harrow to cover over the freshly sown flax seed, the perfect job for a pair of farm horses to undertake on a wartime farm.

The can be no doubt that the number of horses on British farms was in decline towards the end of the 1930s. It is difficult to determine the exact ratio of horses to tractors at the outbreak of war, and it varied over the country, yet it seems reasonable to state that there were at least 10 working horses for every tractor in 1939.

Horses were still an exceptionally good form of power with which to make hay, something that could be fed to both cattle and sheep in the winter months. Horses would also survive on the hay so they very much paid their own way on the farm. Over tricky terrain – such as steep slopes or wet ground – they were still better to use than potentially cumbersome and heavy tractors. They were therefore still considered crucial to the war effort on farms, which is reflected in the fact that they took precedence, alongside dairy cows, over beef cattle, sheep, pigs and poultry when it came to the issuing of rations in the form of concentrates (milled cereals and beans).

THE BRITISH PERCHERON

One particular breed of horse that had become popular with British farmers was the Percheron, which took its name from the La Perche region of Normandy in northern France. Our familiarity with the breed was a result of World War I, when British army officers were particularly impressed with the Percheron's strength, aptitude and versatility. The English shire horse and the Scottish Clydesdale both have a characteristic "feathering" on their lower legs – long hairs that grow down over the hooves. In the heavy clay soils of World War I battlefields, this was to cause them serious problems as they struggled to cope with the ever-present mud and wet. The clean legs and tough feet of

the Percheron were a great attraction to the British, so much so that a contingent of buyers was sent over to France to purchase breeding stock with which to supply the army. At the end of World War I, the products of this army stud were sold off to British farms, where they took to all manner of farm jobs with due diligence, earning themselves a great many supporters in the process. The British Percheron Horse Society was founded in 1918 as a consequence, and it has been going strong ever since.

For us, a pair of Percheron horses proved the perfect form of motive power to harrow in our flax seed, following closely behind the tractor and seed drill, to work in the freshly sown seed. As I was driving our new Field Marshall diesel tractor, we could have used our petrol-powered Fordson N tractor. However, we were struggling with our petrol ration (in both wartime and 21st-century terms!) So it made perfect sense to use horses for a job that they could do just as quickly and efficiently.

The clean legs and tough feet of the Percheron were a great attraction to the British.

DAIRY

» PETER GINN

Below: The last of the imported feedstuffs. I wonder how many farmers must have had sleepless nights worrying about not being able to feed their livestock.
Right: 1 Cutting material to ensile. **2** Cutting wriggly tin the easy way. **3** Lining up the holes. **4** An oil bath of nuts and bolts. **5** Fixing the silo together. **6** A protective layer of straw. **7** Filling the silo. **8** A selection of beet tops. **9** Yum yum!

Due to the war in the Atlantic, huge pressure was placed on the convoys bringing over supplies, which led to a lack of imported bovine feed. This, coupled with a shift in farming from pasture to arable land to meet the demand of staple crops in Britain, meant that there was a reduced ability to sustain a herd of cows.

FEEDING HUNGRY CATTLE

Milk, however, was still very much in demand, so to meet government expectations, farmers had somehow to nourish their dairy. This was especially tricky through the harsh winter months when they would normally be reliant upon imported feed.To this end, the government ran a campaign entitled "Make silage. Make sure." encouraging farmers across the country not only to consider silage as a winter fodder option, but also to be creative about the organic materials that they ensiled. Farmers were generally dubious about silage, and there was by no means a universal uptake of this "scientific" practice, but there was a significant and steady increase of silage-making during World War II, which carried on after the war years.

MAKING OUR SILO

To make silage, one needs a crop to ensile and a container in which to ensile it. We started by thinking about our silo, which needed to be structurally sound to last the winter, as well as airtight and watertight to allow the pickling process to take place. The government literature at the time talked about using sisal paper, which is made from layers of brown paper and tar or pitch. It came in rolls and could be used to line a simple wooden post-and-wire container. There were also suggestions of using railway sleepers or bricks to build a structure, of converting an area

Farmers were encouraged to be creative about the types of organic materials they ensiled to create much-needed winter fodder for cattle.

of an unused barn into a silo, or of constructing circular containers from wriggly tin (corrugated iron). We opted to use the wriggly tin method, as we knew we could scavenge enough odd pieces from within the hedgerows and behind the buildings at the farm, and many of the pieces still had bolts in them, which could also be reused. We ended up with a mix of materials, with some sheets made out of heavy iron and others from aluminium. (During the war, metal was collected to aid the war effort, however much of this was subsequently dumped – see page 219.)

Bolting the pieces together was initially a struggle, but as the silo took shape, the task became easier and we found we didn't need the supports we had scavenged. We lined the base with straw to keep the mud away from the contents and also to prevent listeria. We then had to fill it! Putting ourselves in the shoes of a wartime farmer, we turned to our land and looked to anything we could lay our hands on. Using scythes, we started collecting nettles and grasses from any patch of land on which they were growing, as well as getting hold of sugar beet tops and fodder beet tops. It is amazing how little space these plants take up once cut and slightly wilted, and then trampled and pressed into the silo.

WHAT WOULD RESULT?

Once we had filled the silo, we put another layer of straw on top and sealed it with a heavy layer of clay (of which we have an abundance at the farm) to make the contents airtight, and placed a roof over it to make it watertight. We then left the silo to work its chemical magic. During the ensuing weeks we watched in amazement as the clay sank to almost the halfway mark, despite the fact that we had trampled and compressed the material as much as we could when loading the silo.

Above left: Alex gets close to one of our dairy cows.
Above: Dishing up the last of the feed.
Right: Encouraging our calf to feed from a bucket rather than a teat.
Below: Removing the vacuum milking machine after it has done its work. Between cows, the machine is thoroughly cleaned to prevent the transfer of disease.

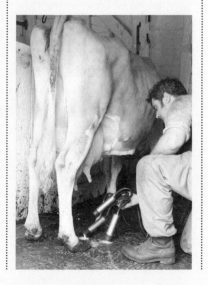

We were slightly dubious when we cracked the silo open, as we had no idea how successful the experiment had been. We were armed with a silage sampling stick – an iron shaft with a sharp metal barbed point that is thrust into the contents to pull out a pinch of ensiled matter. We also had a leaflet entitled "Silage: how to make and feed it". This had a handy table of Faults, Causes of Faults, and Remedies, which we used to judge our silage. I would say that we made pretty reasonable silage, although the quality did vary – but then so did the materials that we ensiled. At least when we fed it to the cows they ate it.

MILKING AND DAIRY PRODUCTION

Prior to the war, Britain consumed on average half a pint of milk per person per day. By 1943, milk production had fallen as a result of the plough-up policy and the lack of imported feed stuffs for livestock. However, this only a fall of 4 per cent and Ministry of Foods concerns led to an increase in the quality and safety of milk. This, coupled with the fact that less milk was being used in manufacturing food, meant that direct consumption of milk increased by 30 per cent, with many of the poorest people in Britain having a lot more milk than they did before the war, especially after the introduction of the National Milk Scheme (which was later made largely redundant due to a rise in wages). The scheme gave expectant and nursing mothers and all children under five a pint of milk a day. Free milk was also given to households where the combined income was below 40s.

MECHANIZED MILKING

During the war, many farms with large herds did all their milking by hand, but our farm had a mechanized milking machine which, through the use of a motor, creates a vacuum that extracts the milk from the cow. It always amazes me how easily animals can get into such a routine. The cow comes in to the shed to be milked at the same time every day, and the action of milking provides the cow with relief. However, in order to encourage and capitalize on milk production, calves are bottle-fed about two days after being born, so they get the initial colostrum from the mother but the amount that they consume can be regulated. They can then be allowed to grow into dairy cows themselves (assuming they are female), with skinny bodies and large udders, to increase the size of the herd.

During the war, many farms with large herds did all their milking by hand.

SHEEP: THE HAMPSHIRE DOWN

» ALEX LANGLANDS

The chalk downland of the southern counties of Sussex, Hampshire, Wiltshire and Berkshire have given birth to a rich variety of sheep breeds over the centuries. To the communities in the valleys, the vast tracts of open downland draped in diverse grasslands represented a valuable resource upon which to graze shepherded flocks.

Whilst the Wiltshire Horn was bred for its meat, the Berkshire Nott, Old Hampshire, and the "south Down breeds had all evolved to convert thin downland grass into wool for market. In the 18th and 19th centuries, however, changes were afoot in agricultural practices and a new breed was required that could not only work well on the exposed and open downland but also fatten quickly on arable fields. This was because farmers were increasingly looking to sheep to provide fertility through their dung to increase yields in cereal crops. To do this, they would sow a crop of turnips upon which to "fold" the sheep. Sheep manure would, in turn, add precious nutrients to the soil.

After several decades of selective breeding, by the mid-19th century what has come to be known as the Hampshire Down breed emerged, and it is likely that it drew on the best attributes from its neighbouring breeds, with its stock ancestry in the Old Hampshire and Berkshire Nott. Its ability to produce meat almost certainly came from the Wiltshire Horn, and its stocky and compact frame from the South Down breed from Sussex. With its dark browny-black eyes, ears and muzzles, dense fine fleece, and stocky build, the breed had an excellent ability to thrive on the hills, along with a fantastic

capacity to convert excess food into meat. It is difficult to overstate the importance of this breed to south of England farming. The soils of chalk downlands are famously thin, and the use of the Hampshire Down in rotations to provide crucial fertility through its manure was ultimately what made growing cereals on the same ground year after year possible.

It pained me to see an animal that had been of such great use to the farmers and folk of southern England became so redundant in Britain's time of greatest need. Fattening for meat was out of the question. The food could just as easily feed hungry people directly. Also, the value of wool plummeted as Britain did what it had in World War I and bought the entire Australian yearly wool clip at a fixed price.

LOST SHEEP

Sheep numbers overall fell by as much as 42 per cent in some arable counties, whilst the decrease in the hillier counties was only between 15 and 22 per cent. Towards the end of the war, the loss of the fertilizing properties of sheep over arable land caused concern for the Ministry of Agriculture. Yields of cereal crops were falling as the soil became exhausted, and there was a strong feeling in the farming community that sustainable food production could only be based on a form of mixed husbandry, with animal manure vital to keeping the land in good heart.

The sharp decline in numbers affected many of the rarer breeds, and from the southern counties, the Wiltshire Horn and the South Down were hit particularly bad. Their avoiding extinction is down to the efforts of a few dedicated breeders. The Hampshire Down didn't fare too badly – the dedicated improvement programme of the early 19th century put it in good stead for a post-war role as a meat producer.

> It pained me to see an animal that had once been of such great use to the farmers and folk of southern England, now redundant.

PIGS: THE HAMPSHIRE HOG

» ALEX LANGLANDS

Two landscape types spring to mind when one thinks of Hampshire. The first is the rolling open chalk downland one is confronted with upon entering the county from the north. The second is best approached from the south and is characterized by heathland and forest and remnants of what were once vast tracts of woodland which remain today in the form of the New Forest and the lesser-known Forest of Bere (a short distance to the east of our farm). If sheep are synonymous with the open downland, then the animal that best exploited the dense woodland pastures of southern Hampshire was the pig.

FEEDING AND BREEDING

For centuries "pannage", a form of woodland grazing, was a common right enjoyed by the pig farmers of Hampshire, and in the autumn months, when the ground was thick with acorns, beech mast, chestnuts and hazelnuts, herds of pigs would be turned out into the forests to fatten up prior to slaughter, salting and curing. At its peak in the 19th century, in the New Forest alone some 5,000 pigs would be turned out every year. This right, known as "Common of Mast", was still enjoyed during the war by New Foresters (albeit in significantly fewer numbers).

The impact this rich nutty diet has on a lean, free-range pig is to create the most awesome-tasting meat, leagues apart from regular factory-farmed pork, and this may well have been the reason for its regional notoriety. As early as the 18th century, the men of Hampshire have been referred to, somewhat jocularly, as "Hampshire Hogs" as a result of the county's association with its porcine heritage.

Today, the association is continued through what is known as the Hampshire pig, a breed that shares the characteristics of its cousins, the Wessex and Essex Saddlebacks. They are medium in size and black all over, apart from a "saddle" of pinkish skin that runs down over their front legs. Where the Hampshire differs from other saddlebacks is in its

> For centuries "pannage", a form of woodland grazing, was a common right enjoyed by the pig farmers of Hampshire.

Right: The Saddleback pig, a popular pig amongst Hampshire farmers in the 19th and early 20th centuries but a breed that suffered a decline in numbers as a result of the war.

Above: Old English piglets were lively and quick to fatten, but competition with humans for rationed food led to a decline in numbers

retention of pointed and alert, rather than floppy, ears, giving it a friendly appearance, and this may indeed represent a throwback to the boars and hogs of the ancient Hampshire forests.

AMERICAN COUSINS

The redirection of feeding stuffs for human and dairy cow consumption during World War II really took its toll on commercial pig farming, and by 1945 numbers were 50 per cent lower than they had been in 1939. As early as 1943, concerns over the national breeding stock were voiced by ministers and farmers alike, with the prospects of recovery in the post-war years looking grim. However, the most catastrophic event to impact upon the rich variety of native pig breeds was the recommendations of a committee set up at the end of rationing in Britain, advising on the best way to make the UK's pig industry internationally competitive. In their report, published in 1955, they advised that, for the benefit of commercial markets, a limited number of breeds should be used for breeding. The results of this advice were to have serious consequences – within 10 years, four county breeds were extinct. The Wessex and Essex Saddlebacks were merged into the British Saddleback, and the Hampshire pig hung on simply because so many had been exported to the USA the previous century and could be re-introduced.

CHICKENS ON A WARTIME FARM

» ALEX LANGLANDS

Today, keeping chickens is popular amongst people who live in the countryside, but also among those in suburban and city areas. There can be little doubt that this modern popularity owes much to the encouragement given by the Ministry of Food to poultry-keeping in the war years.

Egg and meat production had been one of the few sectors of British farming that was doing reasonably well during the inter-war period. Of the £285m per year that farming brought in to the national economy, a respectable £30.4m came from the poultry industry, placing it third behind milk production (at £74.4m) and beef production (£41.5m). With the outbreak of war, however, poultry-keeping found itself in a far less secure position. As it was for pigs, commercial chicken-keeping relied primarily on concentrates such as cereals and beans for feeding. These were obviously feeding stuffs that could have gone, in a desperate situation, to feeding people rather than animals. Yes, chickens produce eggs and meat, but in the conversion of grain to what could now be deemed luxury foods, there was a calorific loss of some 70–90 per cent.

CHICKENS GO TO WAR

Despite this, the government was keen to ensure that the supply of eggs to the nation didn't dry up, and in September 1940 it established the Domestic Poultry Keepers' Council. Its aim was to provide guidance and encouragement to back-yard poultry-keepers, the same kind of people being targeted by the Domestic Food Producers' Council and the "Dig for Victory" campaign. Essentially, the government didn't want domestic house and food waste to go unused, and whilst membership was not compulsory, registering with the Council allowed the government to make more effective use of what little rations were available.

For us on the farm, it was very much a case of letting the chickens fend for themselves.

In general, the Domestic Poultry Keepers' Council can be seen as something of a success story, as in its first year it recorded a membership of 791,000. Furthermore, by 1945, this figure had increased to 1,369,000 members who reared just over 12 million hens. Hence, the foundation stones were laid for popularity of chicken-keeping today.

CHICKENS ON A DIET

Despite the setting up of the Domestic Poultry Keepers' Council, things weren't necessarily easy for back-yard birds. They certainly weren't without their own war to fight in the battle to lay eggs. Like humans, the national chicken population, whether in backyard or commercial farm production, was placed on a rationing scheme. The Ministry of Agriculture had arrived at a food allowance based on a total of one-third of the numbers of chickens kept before the war, and for the summer months this ration was to decrease further to one-sixth of pre-war numbers. Each chicken, therefore, was essentially getting, in the cold winter months, one-third of what it had been enjoying before war broke out. For garden poultry-keepers,, the goal was to ensure that the maximum use of house and garden waste was being made for the sake of egg producers. For us on the farm, it was very much

Poultry-keepers and the poultry themselves were going to have to up their game.

Left: A supply of electricity to the farm's outbuildings enabled the use of a wartime hatchery and brooder cover. This allowed us to prevent the few chickens we had from going broody so that they would continue laying eggs.

Below: Egg collecting everyday - the perfect job for some willing evacuees.

Far below: At the height of summer, the farm's ducks and chickens were producing a healthy basketful of eggs.

a case of letting the chickens fend for themselves, and forcing them to forage in the hedgerows and fields to supplement their meagre government-sanctioned diet. It has been calculated that for poultry farmers a food ration based on one-sixth of pre-war chicken numbers equated to having two birds less per acre. Times were going to be hard and, if egg numbers were to be kept up, poultry-keepers and the birds themselves were going to have to up their game.

Things, however, were to get worse and in 1942, it seemed inevitable that both pig and poultry keeping would be dealt a blow so severe that recovery would prove extremely difficult. The situation arose because of continuing shortages in human food – particularly in wheat for bread. To solve the problem, the Ministry of Food proposed that the level of flour extracted from the milling of wheat be increased. When wheat is milled, all of the bran, husk and the coarser elements of the wheat grain are separated from the soft pure flour that is used to make bread. Increasing the extraction rate from 80 per cent to 85 per cent would lead to a 5 per cent increase in the availability of Britain's bread, at the minor cost of it being marginally less palatable. Critically for poultry, which were fed on the by-products of the milling process, this represented a significant decrease in their ration. Dairy herds and pigs were also largely dependent on fine-milling offal, and because the Ministry of Food was not keen to see any dip in the production of milk, this shortage of 650,000 tons of feed was to fall squarely on the shoulders of the pig and poultry world. It was calculated at the time that this would result in a loss of 20,000 tons of bacon and 670 million eggs per year. To a nation that prided itself on its traditional bacon and egg breakfast, this would be a bitter pill to swallow and the government realized very quickly how badly this might affect morale.

THE DREADED DRIED EGG

But what could they do? Desperately, they considered their options. Allocating shipping space for animal feed from the USA to make up the shortfall was a possibility. Another option was to simply ship in the shortfall of meat and eggs, but in both instances extreme pressure was already being placed on the shipping capacity. Eventually, all the government could do was to issue coupons for the release of 87,000 tons of maize from their central reserve of feeding stuffs. Maize doesn't have anywhere near the nutritional value of fine-milling offal, and as a consequence of the desperately cold winter of 1942/43, the numbers of eggs being produced dropped from a pre-war high of 3,837 million to a mere 1,942 million in 1943. As the situation improved, numbers rose to 2,401 million eggs per year by the end of the war, but for many kitchens throughout the nation, the horror of dried egg powder had become a distinct reality.

BEEKEEPING: KEEPING A HIVE

» ALEX LANGLANDS

Right: A shaded glade made for the perfect location within which to beaver away at my skep.

Below: The skep-maker's tools of the trade. Left to right: apple-wood needle, turkey leg bone needle, pen knife, hand knife, girths, pith-scraper and spar hook.

Far below: The finished skep hive. I constructed a brood chamber to house the laying queen, on top of which I secured a chamber to collect honey from. Straw bales and a nettle thatched tin roof provide perfect shelter.

Bees were ideal wartime livestock. They required only minimal feeding, and a colony could often be acquired for little or no payment. A wartime bee-ready hive and basic equipment cost approximately £7 10s, and a colony of honeybees could be bought for between £2 and £4. If you made your own hives, you were able to buy a pound's worth of timber and plans without needing a permit – a real benefit with wood purchases subject to regulation. It was quite common to see two or three beehives in a domestic garden or an allotment. Bees helped to pollinate your crops, and selling excess honey provided supplementary income.

Thanks in part to the British Beekeepers' Association's lobbying for honey to be recognized as an important foodstuff, in 1943, the Ministry of Agriculture awarded wartime beekeepers an extra sugar ration with which to feed their bees. This extra ration comprised supplies of sugar "not exceeding 10lb per colony" that should be used to keep beehives going through the winter, with an additional 5lb "for spring feeding".

GREEN HONEY

But gaining this extra ration was not automatic and, to stop illegal claims, the police were required by law to check that beekeepers were actually looking after the number of colonies for which they were claiming. When it was suspected that most of the extra sugar wasn't reaching the bees, because the resulting honey crops were so small, someone had the bright idea of colouring the beekeepers' sugar ration green to prevent it from getting onto the black market. This was soon stopped when the bees started to produce green honey!

During the war, over a million hives were active in the UK. However, when sugar came off-ration in 1953, the number of maintained hives dropped until it reached the current level of around 250,000. Increased use of pesticides in agriculture and the destruction of hedgerows to make larger fields also made life difficult for bees and beekeepers.

MAKING A STRAW BEE SKEP

With sugar heavily rationed during the war, honey found itself hugely in demand by local authorities, and in 1943 the Ministry of Food issued an extra sugar ration to beekeepers to feed their colonies throughout the winter months. By doing this, a greater number of bees would survive a harsh winter and so produce even more honey the following summer.

Many allotment holders and gardeners wanted to cash in on this incentive and could purchase wooden hives in kit form. I, however, decided to go for the more traditional form of hive. One thing we didn't lack on our farm was straw and brambles, and both those materials could be cunningly stitched together to make a good old-fashioned bee skep.

The huge increase in cereal-growing during the war meant there was a glut of straw, and farmers were trying to find innovative ways of using it by either rotting it down for manure (by adding ammonia and quick lime) or by building with it in bale form. Although a skep would use only the smallest amount of straw, it was nonetheless a legitimate use of time and materials and, if successful, would provide us all with a morale-boosting sweet treat.

Making a bee skep is actually rather easy once you get started. Perhaps the most difficult aspects of the whole process are sourcing the tools and preparing materials. Firstly, you will need a small spar hook or a hand knife, and both will need to be as sharp as you can get them. You will also require some kind of needle for the stitching. I found a curved branch of apple wood with a concave recess cut in one end to be ideal, but a piece of copper pipe with the end cut off at an acute angle would probably be more durable. The leg bone of a goose or turkey cut in much the same way makes for a more traditional tool. You will then require at least one "girth". A napkin ring, provided it is not too wide, could work well but cutting the first couple of inches from the fat end of a cow horn will give a more traditional tool. I clamped a branch of larch wood and gauged out a 35mm (1½in) hole for my girth and employed two in the making of my skep.

Getting the bramble cane right is the most crucial thing and this starts with selecting the right material. What you need is the long thick cane that grows in the middle of a tall hedgerow, shoots directly towards the light and then cascades out the top of the hedge, sprouting side branches as it falls. Once you've snagged your clothes and scratched your hands and face trying to get to the stuff, cut it into 1.5m (5ft) lengths to transport back to your favourite work spot.

WORKING THE BRAMBLE

Splitting is the most difficult part of the process and can result, certainly in my experience, in a good deal of cursing and a scatter of uselessly short material. However, with patience and the development of good technique, you should be able to split each length down into 5mm (¼in) strips (see photo no. 1). Removing the pith from the middle is a tedious job but made much easier by soaking the split lengths for a good few days beforehand. If you want to use the bramble cane with the bark on, for the sake of a rustic appearance, don't soak for too long. If you want a cleaner finish, however, once the pith is removed, the cane can be "stropped" to loosen the bark. This technique is very much like the way in which one makes ribbons curl as a decorative feature of a freshly wrapped parcel. Run the back of the knife down the inside of the cane, secured by hand and foot at each end, which will make it curl up and shed the outside bark. Your bramble cane is now ready to use. Remember, the better the cane you make, the easier your job is going to be in the long run!

SORTING THE STRAW

You will need traditional long straw for this job, and a friendly thatcher should be only too pleased to part with a sheaf or two for a drop of scrumpy cider. Clean up the straw by cutting off the ears and any leafy matter and ensure that it is damp and pliable. Take a small handful – about 35mm (1½in) thick – and stagger the ends. I'm right-handed so I held these staggered ends in my left hand and started my cane bind with my right (see photo no. 4). Having secured the cane end and wrapped it round 5 or 6 times, the straw is then twisted round on itself so that the next loop of cane can be threaded through the third or fourth loop (see photo no. 5).

STITCHING IT UP

Having done this, the skep is now ready to be stitched together. Insert the straw through the girth and make sure at all times that it is replenished as material is worked into the skep. You'll find your own technique in time and if the materials are to hand, you should develop a nice rhythm. The shape of the skep is very much dependent on the angle at which you secure to the previous bind. You might want to start parallel with the first few rounds to get a flat-ish top before coming in at a slight angle to dome the sides. It is really up to you to create your own shape. Once happy with the size and shape, taper off the straw at a point corresponding to where you began. I stitched a length of willow around the base of my skep to stop the bottom from weathering and to deter nibbling mice. You're now ready to go out and catch your swarm – but be careful and make sure you're well wrapped up!

Right: 1 Splitting the bramble cane. Rather than drawing the knife towards you, for better control use a twisting technique to open the split out. **2** Slicing the pith from the split cane. Always be sure to work away from your hands with a razor-sharp knife. **3** Separating the cane from the bark wood. **4** Beginning the first bind. **5** Six binds should suffice for the first roundel. **6** To create the first roundel, twist the straw in an anti-clockwise direction. **7** Threading the cane through the needle to stitch the first loop. **8** As you complete each round, extra loops may be needed to increase the number of binds per round. **9** Twisting the straw and manipulating the cane to secure the bind is important to keep the whole structure taut.

MAKING HONEY

» ALEX LANGLANDS

Right: Removing the honey and wax comb from the frame using a spoon is a surprisingly hard job.

Modern beekeepers extract honey from the combs in their hives using an extractor, which operates like a domestic spin drier. With this modern method, the wax comb, within which the honey is stored, stays intact and can be returned to the hive for the bees to refill.

However, it is more than possible to extract honey by hand. Hold a warm 32°C (90°F) honeycomb with capped cells at 60 degrees to the horizontal, with the bottom end sitting over a sturdy bowl. Using a serving spoon, scrape the comb and honey from the frame into the bowl. This mix can be pounded with a pestle to make a finer grain, poured into a muslin cloth and hung over a bowl to filter out the honey from the wax. Although I scraped honey and wax from a hive frame, the loose comb cut from skeps can only really be extracted using this method because skeps do not contain fixed frames for the bees to work from.

I'd always been taught that skep beekeeping was bad for bees. It has been argued that to get to the honey, the colony had to be destroyed, and without being able to inspect the interior of the hive the health and welfare of the bees couldn't be checked. I was beginning to change my mind, though, on this. Actually, through the construction of a brood chamber (see picture on page 162, far below), the laying queen and her brood could be safely excluded from the honeycomb due for extraction. Also, skep beekeeping encourages the bees' natural desire to reproduce, whereas hive and frame beekeeping suppresses this. Cutting honeycomb from a skep does mean the destruction of the wax comb, meaning more work for the bees, however, the risk of disease-carrying from comb to comb is erradicated. So, skeps aren't all that bad.

Above top: Having pounded the honey and wax comb in a bowl, it can be poured through a muslin cloth for filtration.
Above: In theory, the honey drips through the loose weave of the muslin cloth whilst the wax is kept inside.

RABBIT FARMING

» PETER GINN

"Run rabbit, run rabbit, run, run, run,
don't give the farmer his fun, fun, fun,
he'll get by without his rabbit pie,
so run rabbit, run rabbit, run, run, run."

This 1939 song sung by Flanagan and Allen remained in the national consciousness long after the war ended. Its popularity was entrenched as it was used to poke fun at the initial bombing raids of the Luftwaffe, which were rumoured to have killed a couple of rabbits on the Shetlands. It also reflected the wartime love affair between Britain and the rabbit.

Rabbit concerns started across the country because they were a good source of meat (a scarce resource during the war) and they could be reared on relatively little. To start a rabbit concern, one needs a doe (female) of at least six months and a buck (male) of at least seven months. Mating is a short affair, and the gestation period is only 30 days. At the end of this time, you will have a litter of blind, bald and helpless kits, ranging anywhere between four and twelve in number. It takes at least five weeks to wean the babies from their mother and a further month or so until they are ready to be butchered, when they make a very tasty and manageable meal high in protein and low in fat.

EASY TO HANDLE

A rabbit will generally live between nine and twelve years and they are herbivores, eating grass and plants so can easily be sustained on kitchen scraps or be reared in a hutch moved around a grassy area. Rabbits are a ruminant and poo two types of dropping. The first is the type we've all seen when walking in the countryside: hard pellets consisting of undigested plant matter (not too dissimilar to horse manure). However, back at the burrow, rabbits produce soft pellets that they reingest. I was lucky enough to be given a lesson in rabbit-rearing by Dr Anne McBride,

Above It may look cute, but this is one of the best protein livestock animals in this country.

Right: Dr Anne McBride, our rabbit expert, giving me a lesson about how best to care for our new charges.

who has studied their behaviour and is an advocate of their role as a livestock animal, because they produced four times as much protein-to-acreage-consumed than cows. With a nine-month breeding season, a single female can produce multiple relatives and, as a man who has been kicked by cows, sheep and goats, I can appreciate why rabbit-rearing (a gentler experience by comparison) was taken up with such gusto during the war.

However, the main reason was the meat. It continued to be a staple of the diet in Britain until the end of rationing in the 1950s, which also coincided with the outbreak of myxomatosis. At this point people began to turn their backs upon the cuts of meat they had had to make do with, and the popularity of rabbit declined. I wonder if we will ever embrace rabbit in the same way as we did during the war? If we do, a little tip: when dandelions are flowering, pick some and dry them – rabbits do like them.

CHAPTER SIX

HOME DEFENCES

During World War II, the British armed forces engaged in a number of conflicts around the globe. However, back at home every man, woman and child fought their own war of rationing, blackouts, staying vigilant, and keeping mum. Never before had the nation united so closely and with so much commitment. It is for this reason that their actions still resonate in our lives today.

It is very easy to give war a purely aggresive, military image. It is perhaps much harder to empathize with the endurance of limited supplies, fear of death, loss of possessions, death of family and friends, and the witnessing of horrors on a near-daily basis. As a pamphlet by the US Government to American soldiers stated: "There are housewives in aprons and youngsters in knee-pants in Britain who have lived through more high-explosives in air-raids than many soldiers saw in first-class barrages in the last war."

LOCAL ORGANIZATIONS

» PETER GINN

A key idea during the war was that everybody "did their bit", which gave rise to a plethora of auxiliary and volunteer organizations. The organizations and individuals are numerous and varied, but they are all summed up by that enduring wartime phrase, "Dunkirk Spirit". The evacuation of troops between 27 May and 4 June 1940 was declared a miracle, and seen in the press as a disaster turned to triumph, made possible by the help of a flotilla of around 700 little boats all "doing their bit".

CHILD LABOUR

The Boy Scouts (formed in 1908 by Robert Baden-Powell, and essential in World War I) had initially taken up warden posts, but the government withdrew their right to ancillary appointment in October 1940 so they contented themselves with building Anderson shelters for those who were unable to and running messages for hospitals. The Girl Guides (founded 1910) performed similar duties to the Scouts, but also took up the call to collect wastepaper for the war effort – a thankless task. They were assisted in this by groups of Cogs. The Women's Voluntary Service (WVS) organized the Cogs scheme, based on the idea that even children could be cogs in the great machine of war with their collecting work. Badges and ranks were awarded to the most successful collectors.

WHAT WOMEN WERE UP TO

Many of the children would have been put on trains at the start of the war by members of the WVS, founded in 1938 by the Marchioness of Reading, Stella Isaacs. Initially an organization that was tasked with educating households to the dangers of air raids and how they could protect themselves, by the Blitz of 1940 the WVS had become the caretakers and facilitators of wardens, fire fighters, victims and refugees, providing

Right: Around our kitchen table with Steve Taylor our A.R.P. man (and sadly no – the tea did not stop him issuing us a fine for showing a light).

Below right: The call for men aged 41–55 would have been 17–31 at the outbreak of the Great War.

The emergency services were obviously stretched during the war so desperately needed extra volunteers.

food and drink round the clock and aftercare. It is this organization and others like it that made sure people didn't go hungry, or thirsty, helped them find loved ones, and finally find shelter after the mass devastation of a bombing raid. To sing their praises is to acknowledge the impact the bombs had. And, of course, there were also the efforts of the WI, which helped feed the nation with their preserving centres, as well as performing other vital functions (see pages 128–31).

The emergency services were obviously stretched during the war so desperately needed extra volunteers both to deal with the added catastrophes and to make up the numbers as previous employees were called up to the armed forces. One of the main dangers that had been identified prior to the outbreak of war was the effect that incendiary bombs would have on a densely populated area. My grandfather was a firewatcher in London and would stand at night on top of a building in the city waiting for the bombs to drop and reporting the outbreak of fires.

AIR-RAID PRECAUTIONS

» PETER GINN

During World War I, Zeppelins and, later, twin-engine Gotha bombers had caused panic and riots. As bombers continued to be developed in the inter-war period, the Air Raid Precautions (ARP) committee was set up in 1924. However, there was much debate as to whether the major threat would be from bombs or from gas. Certainly, the effects of gas must have been burned into the minds of so many who had served in the trenches.

GAS MASKS FOR ALL

It is, therefore, unsurprising that, at the outbreak of war 38 million GC (General Civilian) respirators or "gas masks", made from a single piece of rubber with a plastic eye piece, were issued to men, women, and children. There were also civilian duty respirators designed for people working in the presence of gas, and service respirators for those working in heavy gas concentrations, which gave the same level of protection but had bigger filters so could operate for longer.

REFUGE ROOMS

In addition to the issuing of gas masks, some 40 barrage balloons attached to steel cables and winches appeared above the skies of London, trenches were dug in parks, and instructions as to how to create a "refuge room" were issued to the public. A basement or ground floor room was recommended, preferably without windows, which could be made gas-proof by filling cracks with putty or pasting them over with paper, filling vents with sodden newspaper, taping shut windows and fixing a sodden carpet or blanket over the door with wood and nails. The room would then be equipped with tinned food, paper, paste (for sealing any further cracks), and eating utensils and things to help pass the time, such as playing cards or a book. It should also contain washing facilities,

As the war progressed it became apparent that the major threat was not going to be from gas but from aerial bombardment.

Left and below: As the horrors of war loomed on the horizon people were encouraged to get used to wearing their masks.

Right: Alex and I with our gas masks on. Ours had charcoal filters but many of the period used asbestos.

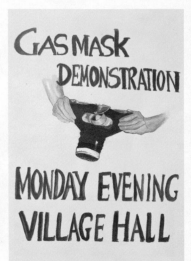

GAS MASK
DEMONSTRATION

MONDAY EVENING
VILLAGE HALL

sleeping facilities, lots of water, and a bucket of sand for fighting fires. Many families living in cities and towns had already made the hard decision at the start of the war to evacuate their children in an effort to keep them safe. In three days, from 1 September 1939, 1.5 million people had been moved to the country. However, as the war progressed, it became apparent that the major threat was not going to be from gas but from aerial bombardment. The best protection against a bombing raid was not to be where the bombs would fall, but for those who had to remain in the cities, some form of air-raid shelter had to be provided.

ANDERSON AND MORRISON SHELTERS
Of all the air-raid shelters, the Anderson shelter is perhaps the best known. Named after Sir John Anderson, then Lord Privy Seal, it was designed in 1938 and sold for £7, though issued free to all households

with an annual income of less than £250. It was a simple flat-pack design of curved and straight corrugated iron sheets. These bolted together, forming a shed-like structure intended to be dug into the ground with a covering of earth at least 45cm (1½ft) deep. It could withstand practically anything other than a direct hit, but had a tendency to flood and didn't keep the noise of the air raids out.

For people without gardens, John Baker designed the Morrison shelter, named after the Minister for Home Security, Herbert Morrison. It was essentially a steel table with mesh sides and base. In practice, it gave very good protection, being engineered to withstand the upper floor falling. Later in the war, terraced houses in London saw large concrete bunkers being built for use by the whole row, but initial brick communal shelters placed along roads designed for public use, upon which these later shelters were based, did not fare very well. They had a tendency to collapse when hit by a pressure wave from a nearby explosion.

On 24 August 1940, a German bomber accidentally released its payload over London. The following night, 80 RAF bombers targeted Berlin, with the first civilian casualties occurring on 28 August. German reprisals were initially aimed at the docks of Merseyside, but soon London found itself in the clutches of the Blitz, and the rest of the country

Left: Digging in the practical and cost-effective Anderson shelters. These submerged refuges would soon have vegetables growing on them.

Below left: Our Anderson shelter.

Above: Later in the war, the government sanctioned the use of London Underground stations as air-raid shelters.

Above right: Although designed by the Duke of Norfolk to withstand a blow by a poacher's stick, city folk would need better protection than bowler hats against the Luftwaffe.

> We will never know the gut-wrenching fear that accompanied the sound of the bombers.

was at the mercies of an escalated bombing campaign. However, very little provision had been made in the way of mass communal shelters in urban areas. The thinking prior to the war was that if large shelters were available, people might go into them and not come out. Also sanitation and safety were a concern.

SHELTERING TOGETHER

The war demonstrated that an entire population can work together, be resourceful, and take the initiative. People established their own large shelters. In London, the obvious place was the tube stations (which had been used during World War I). Londoners bought tickets and didn't leave, but instead came armed with bedding, determined to be safer than they were above ground, prompting the government to make the tube stations official shelters. Other unofficial areas were also occupied, such as "Mickey's Shelter" in Spitalfields, East London (Mickey Davis was an optician who set up a shelter committee) and the Tilbury railway arches in Stepney, East London. Conditions in some of these unofficial mass shelters were beyond appalling, with the stench of the urine and faeces of the multiple nocturnal occupations of 5,000 people filling the oppressively hot air. In contrast, the caves at Chislehurst in Kent had double beds, armchairs, tables, regular church services, and a barber's shop.

In undertaking a project such as ours, as much as we can create a refuge room, enter an Anderson shelter or read about accounts of air raids, we will never know the gut-wrenching fear that must have accompanied the sound of the bombers, or what it must have felt like to emerge from a shelter to see that everything you once possessed lying in a smouldering pile of rubble. What I do know is that if my grandmother had never left her house in London to look for my grandfather, who returned later than usual from a shift fire-watching in the city, I would not be here.

THE ROLE OF THE ARP

» PETER GINN

"PUT THAT LIGHT OUT"

An essential part of Britain's civil defence force during World War II was the officers of the Air Raid Precaution, or the ARP. Officially activated in 1937, it consisted of 200,000 initial volunteers whose role was one of supervision and first aid. They were also responsible for imposing the blackout, which began on 1 September 1939, and they could be heard roaming the streets shouting, "Put that light out". Anyone not seen to be complying with the blackout, either due to refusal to comply or because their arrangement of blackout shutters and curtains was not good enough to stop all chinks of light from getting through, would be warned and possibly fined or worse, if needs be.

The ARP warden (as portrayed in the televsion programme *Dad's Army*) is often seen as an unpopular busybody character. This is a reputation that may have been earned while enforcing a blackout during the period known now as the phoney war. This may also have been the reason why many ARP volunteers began to leave the service for other organizations (especially in London), resulting in a need to reinforce the outfit with paid full-timers and trained individuals in 1940. One fact that does remain is that many people owe their lives to the bravery of these men and the policies that they enforced when they weren't reacting to a crisis, such as a bomb explosion.

GAS MASKS AND BROWN PAPER

At the farm we were visited by Steve Taylor, a man passionate about keeping alive the memories of the 1940s and the Home Front. He told us the precautions we would have had to take against air raids, such as taping up our windows with brown paper to reduce the impact and spread of shattered glass. He explained how we would have been required to carry our identity cards around with us, and he showed us

Above: A roll of Air Raid Precaution Sealing Tape. Have you ever licked a stamp? Try licking several hundred!

Above left: Making the blackout frames for the windows.

Centre left: Fixing blackened card to the frames.

Below left: The well-known tape on the windows that saved many lives, protecting against flying glass shards.

how to use our gas masks. The respirator had rubber straps, which could be adjusted to fit the wearer. It had to be removed by pulling the head harness forward rather than grabbing the metal box (an innovation of the canning industry) containing the charcoal or asbestos filters, as this might have resulted in the cracking of the visor, thus rendering the gas mask useless. Initially, when donning our masks, the seriousness of the situation presented itself to us, but when we exhaled a greater volume of air than the outlet valve could cope with, the mask made a "farting" sound and we were offered a moment of light relief.

One major problem with the gas masks was the reduction of visibility, exacerbated by the little clear visor panel steaming up. To counteract this, many people rubbed soap onto the inside of the eye piece. The masks were originally intended to combat gas dropped by the enemy, but when these bombs didn't come, they served a purpose of combating the fumes generated from the likes of incendiary bombs and the dust that was kicked into the air in the aftermath of a bombing raid.

In September 1944, the tide of war changed and the blackout was downgraded to a dim out. The ARP was disbanded in 1946. It is thanks to them that the bombs that rained down on the UK damaged property far more than they damaged people's lives, health or morale.

THE THREAT OF INVASION

» PETER GINN

Right: Making a ghillie suit from hessian sacks. These were used by the Home Guard as a means of camouflage.
Below: Ever got lost in the country? To confuse the Germans signposts were either altered or removed.
Far below: Similar ghillie suits to the one I made are still used today, especially in a military and hunting context.

Operation **Sea Lion** was Hitler's plan to invade the UK. There is much debate as to whether this would have been successful, but in 1940 both the British and the Americans were convinced it would happen. Churchill tasked Major-General Sir Colin McVean Gubbins with founding Auxiliary Units, answerable to GHQ, but disguised as Local Defence Volunteers or, as they became, the Home Guard.

AUXILIARY UNIT AND NIGHT EXERCISES

Auxiliary Units were first set up in the southern counties most likely to experience invasion, with each cell comprising around four to eight people. The members were usually farmers, known poachers or land owners, as they had local topographical knowledge. Patrols were self-contained and trained in sabotage, demolitions, and assassination, with responsibility for maintaining dumps for weapons and supplies and establishing a hidden base. The patrols had no knowledge of each other and were charged with disrupting and causing damage to an invading force. To this end, the Auxiliary Units spent a lot of time undertaking reconnaissance on local communications and likely nearby headquarters for the Germans, such as country houses. Auxiliary Units members had orders to end their lives rather than be captured alive. The Auxiliary Units were disbanded in 1944, with many members going on to operations in France.

Alex and I found ourselves in an old mine shaft with Auxiliary Unit expert Gerry Sutcliffe planning a night exercise. Our objective was to anticipate the Germans' likely route through the local landscape, setting up an ambush. Plan in place, we moved off into the night, silently following signals on high ground advantage and found ourselves at our desired location. Gerry let off some flashbangs to simulate grenades prior to us popping over the ridge, aiming our weapons and shouting "bang, bang".

HOME GUARD: RECRUITMENT AND TRAINING

In October 1939, Churchill suggested a need for a domestic force to help protect Britain in the event of an invasion. It would also give an outlet to the many people in the country who were being turned down for regular war service, largely due to age. Churchill was not alone in his thinking, so when, on 14 May 1940, Anthony Eden appealed on the radio an appeal for Local Defence Volunteers, people turned up at their nearest police station eager to sign up before the broadcast had ended.

Denounced as a murderous band of *francs-tireurs*, or free shooters (partisans who don't qualify under the Geneva Convention) by the Germans, who said they would execute them if captured, the LDV were not paid and were largely self-funded. These groups of men with arm-band insignia, working all day and staying up all night roaming the countryside with pickaxe handles and fishing knives, morphed into uniformed, disciplined, rifle-carrying platoons known as the Home Guard (their name was changed after a speech Churchill gave in July 1940). Their height of operational readiness was in 1943, which also coincided with their point of greatest bureaucracy, but as the war turned, they were stood down in December 1944 and disbanded 12 months later.

FRIENDLY FIRE

Initially, enthusiasm and weapons could prove a bit of a volatile mix, as happened in Hampshire near our farm. Flight Lieutenant Eric James Brindley Nicolson had to bail out of his aircraft during the Battle of Britain. Nicolson was the only recipient of the Victoria Cross in this engagement – when his aircraft was hit and he was in the process of leaving the blazing, ruined machine, he spotted a second Messerschmitt and returned to his seat to continue firing until it was destroyed. Then, upon parachuting out, he was fired upon by Home Guard members, despite calling out that he was an RAF pilot.

However, training ensued and soon the Home Guard was not only a competent fighting force but also a valuable addition to the civil defence services, aiding with rescue work and incident control. They also manned increasing numbers of anti-aircraft batteries, freeing up regular soldiers for deployment overseas. They took on an essential role of constantly observing the skies and coastlines for indications of enemy attack, and

Left: Training to throw projectiles at the enemy.

Right: Initially a volunteer and self-funded organization, soon the Home Guard became an essential part of Britain's civil defence force.

guarding essential buildings and communications networks. My great-grandfather's Home Guard was tasked with guarding a railway bridge on a train line between London and the south coast.

Despite the fact that "Dad's Army" (so-called because units were comprised predominantly of men over the age of active service) took a lot of flak and were the butt of many jokes, should Hitler and his cronies have ever made it across the Channel, I believe that the Home Guard would have made life very difficult for them. Had Britain not been an island, then our ability to prepare for war would have been grossly reduced. However, we were afforded the time, and to quote Captain Mainwaring, "Come on Adolf – we're ready for you!"

PICTURE **POST**

CAMOUFLAGE
A Home Guard learns a lesson in cover at Osterley Park Training School.

HULTON'S NATIONAL WEEKLY

THE HOME GUARD CAN FIGHT
By TOM WINTRINGHAM

SEPTEMBER 21, 1940   Vol. 8. No. 12

3D

OPERATION STARFISH

THE BLITZ COMES TO THE COUNTRYSIDE

» ALEX LANGLANDS

Right: The Heinkel He 111 was the Luftwaffe's most numerous bomber and inflicted most of the damage done to Britain's cities during World War II.

World War II brought with it a new and innovative type of warfare more calculated and potent than anything seen before. With an unprecedented capacity to inflict desolation and destruction, both sides adopted the tactic of raining explosives down on enemy targets from planes overhead. Chief amongst the targets for aerial bombardment were military airfields, naval dockyards, ammunition stores and industrial centres. In the case of the latter, this brought the terror of high-impact explosives in direct contact with the civilian population who lived and worked around the many factories, power stations, dockyards and railway depots that made up our industrial cities.

HOW MANY CASUALTIES?

In the run-up to the war, the Air Ministry, the War Office, and the Home Office all considered the havoc that aerial bombardment might wreak on their respective concerns. The destruction of Britain's air force would seriously disable its capacity to defend against further bombing incursions, and likewise any damage inflicted on the army would jeopardize Britain's attempt to defend its shores from invasion. For the Home Office, though, the implications of heavy aerial bombardment seemed more immediate and in some senses more sinister. Aerial bombing had not been a large feature of World War I, but the few occasions that it did occur gave the Home Office some statistics to work from. In all, something like 300 tons of bombs had been dropped between 1914 and 1918, with a total casualty cost of just under 5,000 people. With around 16 casualties per ton, the collateral damage in terms of human life didn't seem too overwhelming. However, look a little harder at the statistics: one particularly effective raid in the summer of 1917 resulted in around 800 people being killed or wounded at a cost of 121 casualties per ton of explosives. Therefore, in early 1939, estimates of the tonnage the Home Office believed the Luftwaffe would drop in a single raid yielded frightening results.

A KNOCKOUT RAID

It was thought that a single night's bombardment might involve as many as 600 tons of explosives and result in a potential casualty total, per night, of around 72,000 people. Worse still, there were fears that the German air force, on the outbreak of war, would embark on a massive full-scale air raid, resulting in the dropping of 3,500 tons of explosives in the first 24 hours of the war. This caused some in the Home and War Offices to talk about the "knockout blow" that the German air force could deliver, a blow that would cripple the morale of the British people and cause, ultimately, the surrender of Britain's sovereign powers.

When war broke out, however, there was no knockout blow, and instead Britain had to wait a year before Germany began its bombing campaign which, when it did arrive, was nonetheless vicious and sustained. Various attempts were made to stem the raids but fighter-plane interceptors, anti-aircraft guns, and barrage balloons could only do so much against the multitude of bombers that the German air force was capable of involving in an air raid. For the civilian population, as we have seen, a whole range of air-raid precautions were taken to ensure that minimal damage was inflicted, but, still, there were casualties significant enough to begin to affect morale.

DECOYS AND DUMMIES

The authorities, rather than feeling powerless to do anything about the seemingly unstoppable bombing machine over their heads, devised some of the most ingenious and remarkable ways to thwart the German air force. Tactical deception, in the form of decoy sites, was employed as a strategy by not only the Air Ministry and the War Office, but also by the Home Office.

Put simply, the idea was that imitation air fields, barracks and industrial sites would draw some of the German bombers away from their intended targets, resulting, it was hoped, in less damage and fewer casualty numbers. For the Air Ministry, a complex arrangement of decoy runways, fake huts and hangars and, in some cases, dummy aeroplanes were constructed. The navy attempted to mock up dockyards and harbours through a series of replicated buildings and complexes, all employing simulated lighting, and the War Office followed suit

in attempts to imitate barracks, ammunition depots, fuel dumps, and ordnance factories. For the Home Office, re-creating cities as decoy targets was going to be difficult due to the sheer size of the target. However, there was one way in which they could draw bombers away from city centres, but in adopting this tactic, they would bring the Blitz to the countryside. Those dwelling in villages, hamlets and farms would therefore experience something of the fear and terror felt by their urban neighbours.

FOOLING THE BOMBERS

Operation Starfish takes its name from the initials SF, which were in turn derived from the "special fires" used in the operation. Essentially, these fires were intended to mimic the first wave of incendiary bombs that the German air force dropped on its target as a guide to the following

waves of bombers. The German strategy for its air raids was highly developed and employed state-of-the-art technology so that planes, which bombed at night, could locate their targets. Their system, originally designed for the landing of aircraft in situations where visibility was poor, was able to broadcast radio beams that the planes could fly along on a course to the target site. The pilot would know that he was on course as long as he could hear an audible signal through his earphones. A second radio beam would be broadcast from an alternative ground station and the point at which the two beams crossed would signal the drop-zone. The first wave of bombers would send down incendiary bombs, designed to create large fires, and these would act as beacons to successive waves of bombers. This strategy was used to most devastating effect over

the city of Coventry, where, in the course of two days, 100 acres of the city centre was laid waste, culminating in over 500 deaths.

Air Ministry intelligence intercepted both the beams and various wireless messages concerning the use of them, transmitted between ground staff and air-borne bombers, and they began to put together a picture of how the German system worked. Thus, a limited degree of warning could be given to the target city, anti-aircraft barrages could be organized, civilians mobilized to evacuate, and fire services prepared for the incendiary bombs.

FAKE FIRES

Crucial to Operation Starfish's success was the suppression of these first incendiary fires and, at the same time, the triggering of decoy fires at a site away from

the city centre but close enough to dupe the bombers overhead. Decoy sites were set up all over the country outside of the major industrial city centres, such as Sheffield, Liverpool, Birmingham, Coventry and Glasgow, to name just a few. Southampton, the largest port and industrial centre on the south coast, had its own decoy site and this was situated right on the doorstep of our own Manor Farm on the banks of the River Hamble in Hampshire. The rationale behind the selection of this site lay in an accident of geography best seen when looking at a map of Hampshire. Southampton sits on the estuary of the River Itchen that twists its way up through the county towards Winchester. To the east however, the river Hamble can be observed from above, running in a very similar fashion. By lighting decoy fires close to the estuary of the river Hamble, the plan was, therefore, to try to make the bombers overhead, on course towards Southampton, believe that they were already upon their target and thus cause them to drop their load.

It's difficult to judge the success of Operation Starfish. In many ways, if it saved just one life, then all the effort was worth it. But take a look at a map of Southampton in the late 1940s and it is a picture of devastation. Much of the glorious medieval port was obliterated, and today the city still suffers from a lack of "cityscape" brought about at the hands of the German air force. For us, however, Operation Starfish represented the opportunity to explore an untold story and a little-known aspect of Britain's battle against the Blitz.

PROPAGANDA AND PUBLIC EFFECT

» PETER GINN

World War II was the first major conflict in human history where one side could, theoretically, project information directly into their enemies' homes. Propaganda is often seen as a negative force, but it is just a tool for presenting information. There are three classes of propaganda: white, which comes from an identifiable source; black which one thinks is coming from source A but is in fact coming from source B; and grey, which has no identifiable sources.

WHITE PROPAGANDA

During the war, the government had to establish the best way to sell goods and attitudes to the public. If a governing body knows what the people think and how they behave, then a country's rulers can manipulate its populus. To do this, information had to be collected to rate the effectiveness of the propaganda, and any further propaganda had to be tailored to the prejudices of the public. It's all very well rationing clothes, for example, but first one must know what people wear. To this end, private survey firms such as Gallup and Mass Observation were used to assess impact on morale and carry out market research.

These firms were employed by the Ministry of Information, which had been created at the very end of World War I and was resurrected at the beginning of World War II. It was the Ministry's job both to publicize the war and to control the propaganda, and it had three methods of imposing ideas:

1 Suppress the news and the views that should not be known
2 Release or invent news that should be known
3 Give a few writers special facilities to report, while also restricting them and censoring those without privileges to report

Right: We may refer to this image as "Orwellian" but this is where Eric Blair (George Orwell) got his muse.
Below: It is very rare to meet a spy but most of us love to gossip.

Tell NOBODY – not even HER

CARELESS TALK COSTS LIVES

Propaganda had to be tailored to the prejudices of the public.

THE POWER OF THE PRESS

At the time, Britain was a nation of the most avid newspaper readers in the world. Defence notices (or D-notices) could be applied to anything that was considered a subject that could not be published. Weather was top secret, parachute mines were kept secret for the duration of the war, bomb disposal received no press, and a city bombed during the Blitz could only be named if the government was sure the Germans knew where they had bombed. Some journalists ignored the warnings and printed what they thought the public should know. If one of these hacks was quoted by Goebbels, they could state they were a member of the "Goebbels Club".

Papers relied on advertising, but this dwindled as production turned to the war effort. The Ministry of Information helped make up for this loss, however, as they had a lot to advertise. The "Dig for Victory" campaign, for example, was so deeply entrenched in the national consciousness that it is still remembered today. Posters plastered the sides of walls. In the country not so many were seen, but there would still have been some encouragement governmental drives such as night ploughing.

FILM AND RADIO

During the war, many films, both full-length and short features, were produced. The Crown Film Unit (formerly the GPO Film Unit) was the organization within the Ministry of Information that tasked with making films both for the domestic market and for abroad. Many films were made in a documentary realism style and often sugared the pill, producing propaganda in a covert manner. *Next of Kin* was made to discourage careless talk, *Millions Like Us* celebrated women in munitions, and *In Which We Serve* was Noel Coward's piece for the navy and, of course, the British Public. We watched the GPO film *Spring Offensive*, specifically tailored for the rural market. Our protagonist, a local farmer, takes on evacuees, fixes kit and becomes involved with the War Ag. He visits three local farmers and tells them that they have to plough up their permanent pasture. The first farmer (an early riser wearing shirt and tie) is amerable to the idea; the second farmer (a late riser caught mid-shave) is opposed to the idea, but comes round in the end; the third farmer isn't featured – he is the one who says no and the War Ag have to take his farm.

The BBC had a monopoly on radio during the war. This meant that they could ensure that only "safe" people appeared on shows which could

Below: A very powerful image. Is he 'ssh-ing' his audience from out of the shadows or from beyond the grave?

Far below: The wireless allowed the enemy access to the home and to the mind, making this a very cerebral war.

be pre-recorded and any live shows had a strict script and a producer with a finger hovering over a cough button should a contributor ever feel the urge to scream "peace at any cost". Working with the BBC was a clandestine body, the Political Warfare Executive, which broadcast, every 24 hours, 160,000 words of news in 23 languages to continental Europe. Each station had its own feel and was designed to seem genuine, being produced in the very considered Reithian tradition, enabling falsehoods and Black Propaganda to take on more credence.

BLACK PROPAGANDA

Britain devised black propaganda techniques and justified them because it was seen as the only way to fight the Nazi regime, which was based on lies. Much of the Germans' Black Propaganda exploited pre-existing European prejudices, but one of the most famous German protagonists was Lord Haw-Haw. Initially, the title was used to refer to a number of enemy broadcasters, but eventually one man rose to become Lord Haw-Haw – the American-born William Joyce. His broadcasts began with the phrase "Germany calling ..." and struck fear into the heart of the nation. Joyce was captured after the war and hanged for treason. He had managed to falsely obtain a British passport in order to vote (he was a member of Oswald Mosley's British Union of Fascists) and therefore owed allegiance to the king.

CHAPTER SEVEN
MAKE DO AND MEND

"There is enough for all if we share and share alike. Rationing is the way to get fair shares. Fair shares – when workers are producing guns, aeroplanes, and bombs instead of frocks, suits, and shoes. Fair shares – when ships must run the gauntlet with munitions and food rather than with wool and cotton."
Clothing Coupon Quiz, publicity leaflet produced by the Board of Trade

The shortage of materials to make clothes due to the challenges of importing cotton, wool, and other fabrics, together with the priority given to making uniforms for servicemen and women, led to the introduction of clothes rationing in 1941 – a first in British history. Throw away nothing, and make do or do without, became the order of the day.

The "make do and mend" attitude extended well beyond clothing, too. If some piece of equipment or household tool were broken, buying something new was generally just not an option. Ingenuity and inventiveness were brought to bear in all areas of life, whether that meant turning an old coat into a skirt, using chicken feathers and fabric scraps to create a quilt, or devising a way of generating gas to power a car instead of using petrol.

Go through your wardrobe

Make-do and Mend

SHARE AND SHARE ALIKE

» RUTH GOODMAN

Despite being one of the world's most important manufacturers of textiles in 1939, we were in fact producing only a fraction of the raw materials used by this industry. Northern Ireland produced a reasonable volume of flax for linen yarn and cloth, but all of our cotton was imported, mostly from America. Wool was produced in Scotland, Ireland, Wales, and England, but more was imported, from New Zealand especially. As war cut our imports, arms, munitions, and food took priority, and the supply of cotton and wool dropped drastically.

Meanwhile, many of the factories that had spun and woven that cotton, linen, and wool were turned over to other war work. Those that still spun and wove were working flat out, in the main to produce the materials needed to wage war – for uniforms, parachutes, blankets for servicemen. There was little left to clothe the rest of the population.

Whilst World War I had seen food rationing, the rationing of clothes was entirely new. It began formally in June 1941, with each adult receiving 66 clothing coupons to last them the entire year. This was roughly enough to allow one new set of clothes each. As the war progressed, and supplies got even scarcer than they had been at the start, the 66 coupon allowance was dropped, first to 48, then to 36 and, finally, to only 20 per year. With 66 representing one set of clothes, you can see just how little 36 would have been, let alone 20.

It wasn't just readymade clothes that were affected, but fabric and knitting wool as well. The ration was based upon a scarcity of cloth and yarn to make clothes, not a scarcity of clothes themselves, and that scarcity was just as real if a factory made the cloth into garments or if you made the cloth up yourself at home. Wool, being durable and thus more needed for service personnel, was more expensive in coupons

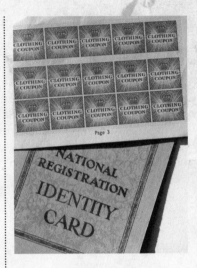

Above: Clothing had never before been rationed, but in 1941 the British public were limited to just one complete outfit a year. As the war progressed, clothing rationing got tighter and tighter.
Left: Severe textile shortages meant that the nation needed to make do with what they already had, to mend and remodel as much as possible.

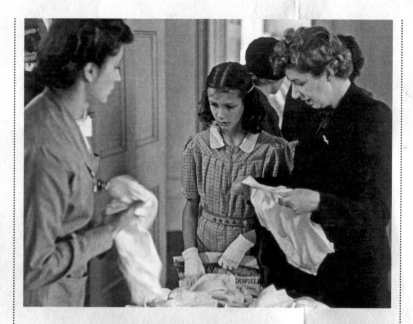

than other materials. A jacket, for example, required 13 coupons if it was woollen and lined, but only six coupons if not woollen and unlined.

Leather and rubber suffered from similar supply problems, meaning that shoes and boots were also rationed. Rubber, relying so heavily on imports, was the scarcer of the two, making pre-war wellies, like the ones Peter had, something to be prized and carefully looked after.

There were a few fabrics that could be acquired off ration. Many people made use of blackout material, and parachute 'silk' was famously and widely used. Many wartime brides wore recycled parachutes on their big day. Second-hand clothing of any sort was also off-ration, and people were actively encouraged to make use of this form of recycling.

DWINDLING WARDROBES

It was, of course, later in the war that clothing became more difficult. In 1939, people had a stock of clothes to varying degrees, but as time went on, these became more and more worn out, and with rationing tightening there was less and less with which to replace those old clothes.

If you are interested in vintage clothing and have a nose around the various dealers and, indeed, museum collections you will quickly notice how relatively few 1930s clothes have come down to us. These were the clothes in people's wardrobes at the outbreak of war. Some were in daily wear and simply wore out. Others, a little older in style, were cut up and remodelled during the war as people did their best to stretch out the clothing ration. Remarkably few 1930s clothes made it through the war unscathed, which is testament to just how thoroughly the population really did "make do and mend".

Older women, and country women in particular, were far more likely to have held on to dressmaking skills.

Left: Second-hand clothes were not controlled by rationing, and children in particular were frequently kitted out entirely from jumble sales.

Right: Sewing classes and sewing machine pools helped women make the most of what was available.

Below: Leaflets and public exhibitions sought not only to encourage but also to help people to 'make do and mend'.

The leaflets published by the Board of Trade gave simple practical advice to a population with needlework skills on how to alter, remodel, and mend what they already had. They included tips on how to turn a pair of men's trousers into a skirt and how to turn two worn dresses into one smart new one. If you were not confident enough to follow the leaflets, you could go along to a class. These were set up all over the country in village halls and community spaces. Some were supported by the Board of Trade, others by the WI, and also by the WVS, all helping women to develop their sewing and knitting skills.

HARDER THAN IT LOOKED

Despite the Board of Trade's assertions that these were simple alterations that anyone could do, they did in truth require quite considerable skills if you were to end up with something wearable. It is no surprise that with materials so hard to come by, many women – who by modern standards were very competent needlewomen – felt very nervous indeed cutting up anything. Take these casual comments on how to revamp an old coat: "With light summer coats, a changeover can often be done by unpicking the facings and revers, adjusting the neckline and seaming the coat up the centre front. The sleeves will probably need taking in a little.'" Hmm. Just how confident are you feeling now about converting a light raincoat into a dress? Younger women, in particular, often needed the help that the classes offered. Older women, and country women in particular, were far more likely to have held onto dressmaking skills throughout the preceding decades as access to ready made, shop-bought clothes had always been more limited for them.

THE CLOTHES WE WORE

Okay I admit it – I like clothes and I like dressing up in them. They seem to me one of the most personal and intimate ways of making that leap into the past. They help you to remember that history is made up of real people who got sore where the elastic cut in, who put on a bit of weight and had to let the waistband out, who fussed in the morning in front of the mirror. Finding the right clothes to wear for a year on a wartime farm was a voyage of discovery for me. I wanted to get it as right as I could. That meant thinking about what was actually in the shops in 1939 in rural Hampshire. It meant getting a feel for what a woman of my age and lifestyle considered appropriate. After all, I didn't want to be mutton dressed as lamb any more than I wanted to look like a stranded townie. What sort of compromises did such women have to make between practicality, fashion and finances? What were the realities of her life?

I spent ages looking at pictures, poking around museums, reading people's accounts of their lives, and then I began with the underwear. The war was not so very long ago really, so unlike with earlier eras, this time I had the opportunity to buy original clothes. I chose to do so with three key pieces of underwear – the girdle, bra and stockings.

DEFINITELY NOT NYLONS

The girdle is a very unlovely garment, the very frumpiest item of clothing ever to be worn by either sex in my opinion. This one was no exception. Made from cotton drill canvas with steel boning and an elasticized front panel, it laces up in two places as well as having hook-and-eye fastenings at the side. It carried the CC41 utility clothing label and was gloriously appropriate for a woman of my age in the wartime years.

Four suspenders hung from the girdle to hold up my stockings. These too, were original – the leftover stock from a shop. They probably didn't sell because they were an unattractive colour and were thoroughly superseded by nylons after the war. Mine were not, most definitely not, nylons. There are so many tales of American GIs giving British girls nylon stockings that you may be forgiven for thinking that every woman had a few pairs tucked in her drawer. You would, however, be mistaken. Nylon stockings were not on sale in Britain before or during the war. It is true that a few pairs did arrive courtesy of American GIs, but most British women's legs were clothed in lisle (cotton) or in rayon stockings. Mine were made from rayon. They were partly opaque and not very stretchy, and had a tendency to wrinkle at the ankle in a truly unattractive fashion, but my goodness they were tough and long-lasting. Quite unlike modern tights and stockings, it was actually quite hard to ladder them and I was able to get months and months of hard, farming wear out of a single economical pair.

Top: A jumper with my suit and blouses allowed me to cope with everything farm life threw at me. My jumper was knitted to a 1942 pattern from *Woman's Weekly*, with fashionably short sleeves and a high waistline. Knitting was hugely popular in wartime Britain. Good and warm, too.
Above: Large practical aprons that were almost overdresses, were an iconic image of wartime womanhood. I think I spent more time in them than out of them.

The bra was a fairly flimsy pink satin affair, as all period bras were – no wires, no padding and not even much elastic, though it did have rather more area coverage in comparison with most modern bras. A wartime bra didn't provide much in the way of uplift, only a light control, with a slight softening of the profile of the bust.

FRUGALITY OVER FASHION

For outerwear I turned to home dressmaking patterns of the period. Most of the original clothing I found was more suitable for town than country wear, and I was struggling to find anything in good enough condition to withstand what I intended to put it through. It is one thing to wear a garment for an afternoon of tea-drinking and quite another to spend a year driving tractors, shifting dung heaps and scrubbing things. So armed with some period patterns, I went in search of fabric. My suit, with a single regulation-sized pleat in the skirt, was typical of countrywomen's wear. Tweed is very hard-wearing indeed, and I knew I would get a year's wear from it with ease. The boxy style was not all that flattering, but it used very little fabric and allowed you to move freely. The blurb on the period pattern made a virtue of its regulation-abiding nature, but the images on the packet showed a much more shapely garment (with a longer and more tailored jacket, and, flared rather than completely straight skirt) than the pattern inside actually made. A practical suit, but decidedly frumpy, just as so many photographs of the period show on countrywomen of my age. The blouse pattern was extremely simple and, again, very frugal. Then we come to my wonderful coat. When I put this on I felt feminine again, hiding all my period frumpiness beneath. Investment in a good coat and hat was a common strategy for those a little more strapped for cash. Whatever you wore at home or did your work in, you could look tidy and nicely turned out whenever you left the house – to go shopping or to church, for example.

Knitting was something of a craze and a fetish with most wartime women. No publication aimed at women was complete without knitting patterns, and a good pattern could be a magazine's main selling point. The young were, if anything, more enthusiastic knitters than the old. Knitting your own designs, rather like hats, gave you a bit of fashion freedom. Yes, new yarn was rationed, but it was so much easier to remodel existing knitting by unpicking it than by trying to do the same with woven clothes.

Below: The pattern was just pre-war, one of Weedon's very popular series and described by them as a coat for country wear – there was also a town coat pattern with a fur collar. I loved my coat. It was by far the most glamorous part of my wardrobe. The hat was a Christmas present. Aren't I a lucky girl!

TWEEDS AND COTTON DRILL

Alex in his search for clothes settled on a tweed suit. Like so many wartime clothes, it has seen some alterations in its time, but still did a sterling service. Whilst superficially a suit may seem to be just a suit, there were two large differences between a suit of the 21st century and one from the war. Most importantly was a huge difference in the weight of the cloth. With so many of us spending the vast majority of our lives now in centrally heated homes and offices, modern men's suits are now made from the very thinnest and lightest of fabrics. Even when they are woollen they are less than half the thickness of a wartime suit fabric. A 1940s suit had to keep its wearer warm in British outdoor temperatures, and, indoor temperatures that were scarcely any warmer. The thick fabric was not only warmer than a modern suit – due to its stiffness, it is better at looking smart. Thin modern fabrics wrinkle and ruck at every movement, while wartime suits just sort of stay there whatever you do. The other basic difference was the waistline. Men's trousers in wartime Britain were up under their ribcage rather than halfway down the hips. Once again, this gave greater warmth and a rather different look.

Peter opted for cotton drill trousers. Unlike tweed, cotton drill can be washed, and it took the wear as well as anything. Cheap, too, He also had a cotton drill "cow coat". It's hard to find a garment more representative of the wartime farm. Popular with people who looked after livestock such coats were hygienic as they could be boil-washed along with the cotton drill trousers and thus well suited to dairy work. But perhaps most exciting were Peter's rubber Wellington boots, usually called galoshes at this time rather than wellies, Peter's were an original pre-war pair that had been well looked after. Rubber galoshes meant dry feet for Peter and much cleaner floors for me, as he could kick them off when he came in, unlike the lace-up boots of Alex.

A 1940s suit had to keep its wearer warm in British outdoor temperatures, and those indoors, which were often scarcely any warmer.

Below left: Peter's cotton drill trousers were a practical choice for someone who knew they were going to get very muddy. Cotton drill can be washed time and time again. Trousers were worn very high waisted, which was good for keeping your back warm.
Below: Knitwear was just as popular for men as for women.
Right: For warmth, Peter turned to a World War I trench coat. Incredibly sturdy, there were plenty of them still around in 1939.

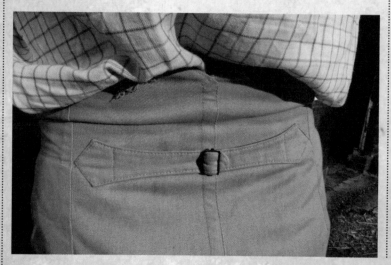

DARNING

You darned socks, darned stockings, darned the rips in your trousers, and darned the worn patches in your apron. Everyone darned, if they hadn't been in the habit of darning pre-war, they would be by the end of it. In essence, darning is the weaving of new cloth using a needle and thread over a hole, rip or thin patch of other fabric. If you were to look in the needlework books of the Edwardian and interwar years, you would find whole chapters on the art of darning, with different techniques for different types of fabric and different shapes of hole.

The Board of Trade's "Make do and Mend" leaflets, however, took a much more belt-and-braces approach. Eager for the population at large to repair and recycle clothing and household textiles as much as possible, they offered advice that was clear and simple. They didn't want to put anyone off when it came to mending. One technique was given that could be applied to anything. The diagrams were fulsome and clear. And if the hole you were faced with was particularly daunting, they suggested that you simply tacked on a patch and darned over the whole lot. Crude, but effective and strong. To further encourage darning, the yarn was off-ration, although there was a limit on how much you could buy at once to prevent people using it for entire knitting projects.

REPAIRS WITH CHARACTER

A really good darn is almost invisible, but even the most lumpy and slipshod of darns lengthens the life of a garment. Peter specializes in this sort of repair. He takes a certain pride in repairing his own clothes – which is just as well at the rate that he rips them – but for some reason those repairs never get any less crude, despite all the practice he gets.

Below: Using a tiny crochet hook, I was able to carefully pick up the dropped stitches when my stockings laddered. Larger holes I darned using my own hair as thread.

A really good darn is almost invisible, but even the most lumpy and slipshod of darns lengthens the life of a garment.

I am rather fond of Peter's darning; it always makes me smile. I don't claim that mine are particularly things of beauty – there just isn't much time for finesse – but it is rather amazing what a simple darn can do for the strength and look of a garment. My stockings, apron and skirt are all darned and I'm hoping that you didn't even notice!

HOW TO DARN STOCKINGS

1 To mend, catch the loop of the running stitch in the hole. Turn the stocking out to the wrong side and fold flat along the ladder.
2 Using thin matching silk thread, start below the ladder and run up one side and down the other, securing the loops at the top and the bottom.
3 Neaten by over-sewing lightly, then turn the stockings the right way out once more. With any luck the mend, won't show.

Below: Good as new.
Right: Keeping your stockings in useable condition could be a time-consuming business in wartime.

LOOKING YOUR BEST

» RUTH GOODMAN

Above: Far from the hairdresser's salon and working outdoors for much of the time in the wind and the rain, my hairstyle suffered a bit. Wartime photographs indicate that I wasn't alone in having bad hair days. Victory rolls are easiest to do if you have thick wavy hair. The rest of us have a struggle on our hands.

Hairstyles and make-up fashions had been heavily influenced by Hollywood in the years running up to the war, and that influence was to continue. Women were keen to emulate the glamorous looks they saw on the silver screen. Actresses like Veronica Lake were particularly copied.

With her mane of blonde hair curling in artful waves to just below her shoulders, and powdered, lipsticked face, she represented femininity with sophistication and sexuality. Achieving such a look required frequent trips to professional hairdressers and dogged use of a range of products. Town girls, with access to the cinema for inspiration and to hairdressers and shops for practical help, were much more likely to achieve the fashionable look than their country compatriots. Many a smartly turned-out young townswoman sneered a little at the decidedly less Hollywood look of women from the countryside. But in turn, there was also disapproval by countrywomen of the artificial look that they saw when they visited town. The Land Girls' handbook contains a warning about wearing too much make-up. Town-bred girls were warned they would look out of place if they didn't tone it down.

HEALTH AND SAFETY HAIRSTYLES

Meanwhile, the practicalities of war were making an impact on women's looks. First to go was the free-flowing mane of hair. War work needed hair either short or pinned-up out of the way. Veronica Lake herself was recruited to popularize "victory rolls" (which kept hair out of the way whilst still giving volume and femininity), in a short propaganda film. But even victory rolls weren't enough for some war work, so women turned to a pre-war fashion for headscarves worn in a variety of turban-like styles. This had been high – and exotic – fashion for a while, so rather than having the modern associations of Mrs Mop that it carries in modern

The government publicly and repeatedly told women that it was their duty to keep up appearances, despite everything, for the sake of "our boys".

Above: The practicality of the headscarf was very welcome.

Britain, the headscarf look actually had a more glamorous interpretation for wartime women. A style developed that combined bits of turban-wearing, victory rolls, and pre-war waves of hair, which could be adapted to the dance floor as well as the cow barn.

KITCHEN CUPBOARD MAKE-UP

As for make-up, it got scarcer. Lots of brands ceased production, though some lipstick manufacture did continue in the interests of morale. The government publicly and repeatedly told women that it was their duty to keep up appearances, despite everything, for the sake of "our boys".

Hints and tips on beauty under difficult circumstances abounded. Face powder could be replaced by laundry starch (that's pretty much all it is anyway). Beetroot juice could be pressed into service as a blusher – laundry starch stained with beetroot juice and allowed to dry before use is actually a very good blusher. Cold creams could be made at home from a little lard beaten vigorously with a few drops of water and scent. Everyone has heard of gravy browning being used to paint stockings on to legs, but it could also be used to darken eyebrows, as could charcoal, and for mascara you just add a touch of lard. If you could spare a little sugar, then sugar and water solution made a reasonable setting lotion for the hair as did laundry starch and water.

HOW TO CREATE A VICTORY ROLL.

① SECTION THE HAIR INTO 3 SECTIONS

② TIE THE BACK SECTION (C) UP & OUT OF THE WAY.

③ TAKE SECTION A OR B

④ BACK COMB THE SECTION TO CREATE VOLUME AT THE ROOTS.

⑤ CURL THE HAIR INWARDS TOWARDS THE SCALP USING YOUR FINGERS.

⑥ SECURE USING BOBBY PINS.

⑦ REPEAT ON THE OTHER FRONT SECTION AND RELEASE SECTION C.

HOMEMADE SHAMPOO

Right: Making soapwort shampoo, which is quite the nicest shampoo I have ever used.

As the war progressed, soap joined the list of rationed goods, which would, of course, have an effect upon personal hygiene. Noticing that one area of the flower garden that I was to dig up in favour of more vegetable-growing was full of soapwort, I decided to have a go at making my own shampoo.

All parts of the soapwort plant contain saponins – the active ingredient. The roots are the easiest to store long-term, so I put them aside for later. Carefully washed, I hung them up to dry for a few days before packing them away in paper bags. Later on in the year, I would be able to get at their saponin simply by soaking them in water overnight, mashing them up and straining out the bits. Meanwhile, unwilling to let any of it go to waste, I made use of the green stalks and leaves to make up the shampoo.

SQUEEZING SOAPWORT

1 Take a good handful of soapwort plants, two bowls and a sieve.
2 Roughly chop up the greens, put them in one of the bowls and bash them a bit with the end of a rolling pin. A pestle and mortar or food processor would do a much better and more thorough job.
3 Without access to these tools, I improvised by tearing the leaves and rubbing them between my hands.
4 Next, pour a kettle of hot water over the bruised greens. As soon as they are cool enough to handle, start squeezing and rubbing the leaves and stalks to help them release that lovely saponin into the water.
5 Bubbles should start to form on the surface, and the texture of the water will began to change; there will be a certain slippery silky feel to it.
6 Squeeze out the soapwort and discard the plants.
7 Pour the mixture through a sieve or colander into the other bowl to get rid of any small bits of plant.
8 You will be left with be a bowlful of warm, vividly green water.
9 Whisking the liquid with your hands will create bubbly water, and this can now be used to wash your hair.

No shampoo I have ever used was quite so vividly green as this. If I had used the roots, the liquid would have been colourless, and it is in this form that it is sometimes used by textile conservationists to clean fragile and precious fabrics that would suffer if conventional soap powders were used. It was wonderful. I can honestly say that my hair has never felt so soft afterwards. The smell was pleasantly, mildly sappy, and I didn't need to use any conditioner. I have quite dry hair and this definitely suited me very well. There was enough cleaning power to get rid of the dirt and grease, but not so much as to leave my scalp tight and itchy, as just about every commercial brand of shampoo does. I am a convert,

HOW TO MAKE A QUILT
POCKETS AND FEATHERS

» RUTH GOODMAN

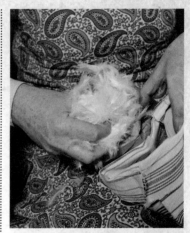

The decision to rationalize our livestock had been a hard one. But as we reduced our poultry numbers, I found myself with an abundance of feathers.

Amongst the many handy tips that I found in the WI handbooks of wartime Britain, I came across quilting suggestions. One consisted of pockets, stuffed with feathers, and all then sewn together. This seemed to me to be practical with winter coming on and the threat of large numbers of people being billeted upon us. It proved to be simple to do and, as sewing projects go, relatively quick.

MAKING THE POCKETS
1 First, sort the feathers, putting all the small soft downy feathers in one basket, and the flight feathers in another. It is only the soft downy ones that you want for the quilt. Anything with a well-formed quill would poke its way out of the fabric of the finished quilt and it is the fluffy downy nature of the feather that makes it such a good insulating material.

2 Next, sterilize the feathers. Batch by batch put them into paper bags to stop them flying all over the place, then bake them in a moderate oven to kill bacteria, but not scorch the feathers.
3 To contain feathers you need a fabric that is very tightly woven, with the threads packed so tight that the feathers cannot work their way out. The traditional material to use for this is ticking, a cotton fabric woven with a stripe. It is the fabric once used for pillows and quilts alike,.
4 Cut the ticking into 23cm (9in) squares. Sew two, right sides together on three sides, to make a pocket. The feathers can be stuffed into each pocket and then sewn together to form a quilt.

You can assemble the quilt bit by bit, as and when feathers became available. I found a piece of ticking in my work basket, but it was too small to make a quilt. Upstairs, I found two pillows in a terrible state. I unpicked the stitching and washed and washed the fabric until it looked respectable.

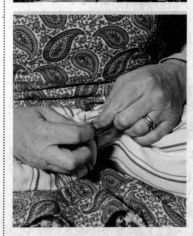

Above and left: Waste not, shiver not. With so many people billeted on us, bedding was in short supply so an extra feather quilt was very welcome.

NEEDS MUST...

» PETER GINN

It wasn't just inside the home that extra ingenuity and resourcefulness were needed in order to make the most of what was already available. Broken machinery had to be mended (often without access to spare parts or other supplies) and forgotten skills needed to be re-learned – the war brought out the Heath Robinson in everyone.

MAKING TILES

One of the aims of this project has been to explore the lesser known elements of rural and domestic life during World War II. Although we have seen pictures of bombing raids, we can never know the fear and destruction they caused and the heartache, the pain or the relief of their aftermath. Often I have wondered what it must have been like to lose your family, your friends, your home, and your possessions in an instant, but I haven't really thought too much about the clean-up operation.

Bricks are fairly resilient and if they do break, they are generally still useable. Tiles, on the other hand, are thin and structurally brittle and, by the very definition of their use as a roofing material, have further to fall. This meant that tile works across the country went into overdrive, operating round the clock to keep up with demand. We needed some tiles to patch up a roof on our farm, so we sought out the expertise of Colin Richards, his son Dan and Mick Kruppa.

PREPARING THE TILES

I dug the clay we needed to make some tiles out of a pit near Bursledon, Hampshire, where a brickworks had been in operation from 1897 to 1974 (it is now an industrial museum). However, the tile-making machine had been moved up to Shropshire earlier in the year, so we found ourselves battling the elements in December on the very exposed Clee Hill.

Top: It was so bitterly cold we kept a small fire burning to keep warm.
Above: Making the kiln. This is the entrance to the fire chamber into which we would spend the best part of 36 hours feeding timbers.
Right: Finishing off covering the fire chamber prior to building the brick container for the biscuit tiles.

The key to a successful burn is in getting the heat to circulate evenly throughout the kiln.

Originally, tiles would have all been hand-thrown but we had a tile-making machine, a Victorian invention. Essentially it was a cast-iron box on wheels, with a tile-shaped slot on one side and a plunger on the opposite side. When the plunger was wound towards the slot the 50:50 clay:sand mix was squeezed out in a large tile shape. Unfortunately, the instructions had been lost and although the mechanism was quite simple, the process of cutting the tiles was trial and error. Once the tiles were made, we had to leave them to dry. The time that this takes is dependent on the weather – in winter this can easily be six weeks or more.

FIRING UP THE KILN

The kiln was quite a simple construction consisting of around 800 bricks forming a long fire chamber, with a compartment for tiles on top. As we created the tile chamber, we loaded it with the dry (and very brittle) tiles stacked on their long edges. I imagine seasoned tile-makers would lose far less than cack-handed Ginn and butterfingers Langlands.

The key to a successful kiln is in getting the heat to circulate evenly throughout it and this is done by four chimneys, one in each corner. The chimneys and the top of the kiln are covered in sand to seal in as much heat as possible. Each chimney is unblocked in rotation, ensuring the heat gets into each of the corners and to the very edges of the kiln.

Prior to lighting the kiln we erected a shelter of canvas, ropes, and poles (cut from the surrounding woodland). This served several purposes. It kept the worst of the weather off both those tending the kiln and, more importantly, the kiln itself, as heavy rains would prolong the firing process. Secondly, it acted as a smoke baffle and a light shield, so passing aircraft would not have seen any activity below.

To start, we kept a small fire in the kiln for several hours (to drive off moisture still in the tiles and any that had been absorbed by the bricks), and very gradually raised the temperature of the kiln. If the tiles were damp and their temperature was increased too quickly, the water in them would expand and the tile explode. In order to tell if there was still water coming off the kiln, we held cold saw blades over the top of it. If water condensed on their surfaces, we knew we had to continue the drying, but when they came back dry, we started to build up the fire and elevate the temperature to around 900°C (1,652°F).

The intensity of industrial fires amazes me. We had to maintain our temperature for around 36 hours, feeding logs into the fire every 15 minutes. (The feeding time varies – the temperatures for our burn were cold but we had a strong wind that almost turned the kiln into a blast furnace.) As the kiln heated, it expanded (we had to fasten an expansion chain around it to maintain its shape) and gaps started to appear. Many of these gaps we plugged using clay, but a few were left as spy holes, allowing us to monitor progress by eye.

THE FINISHED PRODUCT

Once we were satisfied that the tiles were fired, we let the kiln cool naturally, and after a day or so, we were able to open it. The results were better than we expected, with relatively few losses during the firing process (most happened during the loading). As the tiles fire at slightly different temperatures, they had an array of different colours, which would result in beautiful roofs. They were certainly ideal for us.

Right: Loading in the tiles, ready to fire. They may look solid but squeeze too firmly and they will crumble.

PUTTING THE SOCIAL INTO LIFE

One key element of a process like this (especially in the war period) is that no heat is wasted. A kiln burns at a high internal temperature and has a number of external flat surfaces ranging from the warm to the "*&$!& me that's hot!" These surfaces can be used to dry clothes that have got wet in the rain, to cook meals and make endless cups of tea (Italian prisoners of war were known to use the flat tile kiln tops to cook pizzas), but we used the top to make schnapps (meaning any strong alcoholic drink in the European vernacular, rather than American schnapps, which is a liqueur). For this purpose, Colin, a man of many talents, had already distilled apples in a vat, making a fairly rough cider. He then took this cider and put it into a homemade still, consisting of two chambers and a long copper pipe.

When he placed the still on top of the kiln, the cider was heated and the alcohol boiled off, condensing in the pipe and running down into a bottle. The first batch of liquid to be distilled was methanol, which has a boiling point of 64.7°C (148°F). This is the simplest form of alcohol and most dangerous, because if drunk it attacks the optic nerve, leading to permanent blindness.

However, after that ethanol is produced, which has a boiling point of 78.1°C (173°F). We used this to toast the kiln, pouring the liquid on the top and watching the ensuing fireball. It also made a nice tipple to keep even the weariest tile-burner on their toes.

GAS-POWERED CAR

» PETER GINN

The fuel crisis was considered the second battle on the domestic front (after starvation) with gas, petrol, electricity, coal, and water being severely restricted. Propaganda posters claiming "Better pot-luck with Churchill today than humble pie under Hitler tomorrow – don't waste food!" began appearing and cooking techniques that used less fuel were circulated.

During the course of World War II, the fuel shortage led to some inventive alternatives – especially in powering automobiles. In Europe, numerous cars, including half a million in Germany alone, were converted to run off a wood gasifier, a technology that had been around since the beginning of the century. However, in Britain, with petrol supplies cut off, natural gas yet to be discovered in the North Sea, and wood sources not as abundant as they were on the continent, we turned to coal to power some of our automobiles.

When one burns coal in a normal fire, 70% of the calorific value goes up the chimney. As towns grew in the 19th century, more and more of this coal gas, a by-product of coke production, was produced and stored, earning it the name "town gas". Cars in urban areas that were converted

Top: Our vehicular candidate for conversion, 'pre-op'.
Above: The car might have looked very 'Heath Robinson' but it is a perfect example of 'extreme' make do and mend..

to run off town gas usually had a large bag placed on the roof, which could be filled much like a petrol tank, but cars in rural areas had to produce their own coal gas on the go.

THE ULTIMATE MAKE DO AND MEND PROJECT

I helped Colin Richards and Mick Kruppa convert their 1943 ambulance. We started by fixing a platform to the front of the vehicle attached to the chassis, upon which we could construct our mini power plant. On the left, we had a stove with a coal hopper on top of it and as the vehicle moved along, the coal would shake into the fire, which was kept burning with the aid of a fan. The amount of coal is relative to the miles you wish to cover, with the maximum being an estimated 30 before a refill is needed.

The smoke produced in the stove fed into a long, fan-assisted pipe that cooled the contents, which in turn fed into a filter designed to remove any impurities before the gas fed directly into the carburetor. To filter the particles from the gas, we used heather, which is naturally absorbent and has a large surface area. Although a seemingly simple idea, it took a lot of hard work and quite a bit of on-the-go tuning to get the set-up exactly right, but sure enough, when we fired up the stove, and gas began to be driven off the coal, we could start and drive the ambulance. Not only that, but when we stopped, we took out our frying pan, opened the lid of our stove, and cooked up a meal.

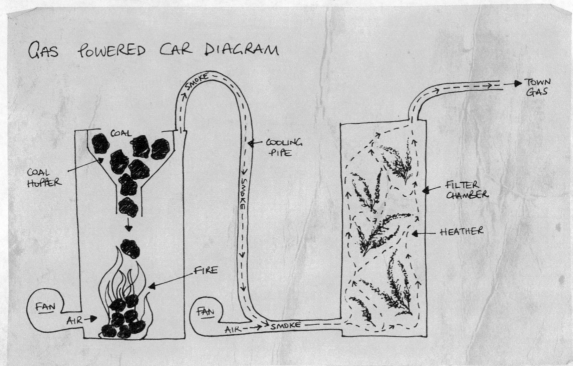

GAS POWERED CAR DIAGRAM

SMOKE

TOWN GAS

COAL

COOLING PIPE

COAL HOPPER

SMOKE

FILTER CHAMBER

HEATHER

FIRE

FAN

FAN

AIR

AIR → SMOKE

SCARING BIRDS
TACTICS AND STRATEGY

» ALEX LANGLANDS

There's a certain type of stress that is brought about by pests. Whether it's moles under the front lawn, rats in the granary or a fox on the prowl, it's a feeling of powerlessness that can only be alleviated by the taking of action. I guess it is the relentlessness of pest control that can really burden the mind, and the knowledge that, despite your best efforts, you can never take your eye off the ball. Most pest problems have an obvious solution. You can poison the rat, trap the mole, and sit up all night for the fox – shotgun at the ready.

FEARLESS FLOCKS

Birds, however, pose an altogether different threat. In my reckoning, they are the hardest to mitigate against. It seems that, no sooner than has the seed been sown in the ground, than they swoop in from nowhere and gobble up the fresh shoots as they sprout. One simply can't be in every field at once to scare the blighters off and even if you did, the moment you turn your back, they're back on the ground scratching around and pecking out your precious crop.

NON-SCARECROWS

One of the most amusing comments ever made to me – one day when I was considering employing a scarecrow on my vegetable patch – came from an experienced farmer and a veteran of decades of bird-scaring campaigns. He informed me that so many pheasants and partridges have been reared by humans that, in erecting a scarecrow, the birds actually think you are feeding them! Also, because in the 20th century there were far fewer people working on the land, when humans were spotted in fields, the birds could be pretty confident that it had something to do with food, whether it be sowing tasty seeds or harvesting them. The iconic image of a scarecrow listlessly propped up against a post with a crow

nonchalantly perched on his arm was beginning to make sense . . .

I decided on something a little more, shall we say, 'explosive' to keep the birds off our freshly sown flax seed just long enough for the emerging shoots to use up the food store in the seeds and for the plants to take root. I'd come across an advert for a bird-scarer in an agricultural magazine of the period and I thought I'd make one from scratch using some old bits of

I'd come across an advert for a bird-scarer in an agricultural magazine of the period and I thought I'd make one from scratch.

tin and timber from around the farm. Fortunately, the key part of the construction, a rope of explosive charges, is still available on the market today, so all I had to do was make a box construction with hinged sides designed to clatter up and down as each charge went off.

Unfortunately, my box construction didn't quite have the desired acoustic effect, the recycled corrugated tin I'd settled on being too twisted and warped to get a flush fit with the rest of the box. The result was that too much of the explosion's force was being diffused through the various gaps.

Nonetheless, the charges themselves went off with a proper and satisfying bang, and although the clattering was more of a polite hand-clap, the tin sides kept the fuse rope and charges dry out in the field.

Far left: The LePersonne bird scarer, as advertised in a wartime agricultural magazine.
Above left: For improved range, I wanted to get as much height as possible from my cobbled-together bird scarer.
Above: A rope of charges is laid down the centre of the box and burns in such a way that every 30 to 40 minutes a charge goes off with a resounding BOOM!

RECYCLING: NOTHING WASTED

» RUTH GOODMAN

Raw materials of almost every kind were in short supply; paper as well as aluminium, animal feed as well as rubber. Everyone in every walk of life was called upon to be careful with what they used and to reuse wherever possible – and when every ounce of use had been extracted to recycle. Nothing could be permitted to go to waste – as 48 million people use a lot of everything, the potential for savings in material use was great, and hundreds of schemes were set up to make those savings.

EVERY LITTLE HELPS

As we have seen, pig clubs (pages 118-121) recycled food scraps that were not fit for people to eat in one form or another – although with a range of recipes available to create appetizing soups from virtually nothing, it is amazing how little that left for the pigs. By 1943, most urban streets had a pigswill bin for the inhabitants to fill. These were regularly collected and their contents boiled up, helping to increase the nation's meat supply with no call upon the small feed stocks.

Children were particularly prominent in the collection of recyclable goods. Paper was just one of several materials that children regularly collected door to door, putting pressure upon all the adults in their lives to swell the size of their hauls. A baby's pram piled high with scrap paper pushed by a couple of eight- or nine-year-old lads was a common sight. Some of these children were organized by their school, others by Scout and Guide groups, still others were entirely independent in their efforts. The *Beano* comic was particularly keen to encourage its readers in waste paper collection activities. Desperate Dan pointed his finger straight out of the pages with the words "You can help Britain by collecting waste paper." Feathers were collected to make pillows for servicemen, scraps of knitting wool for making blanket squares. Silver

paper for recycling was separated from general waste paper. Shoes, boots and clothing were recycled through jumble sales and swap shops. Wood was generally recycled quickly and locally into firewood to eke out the meagre household fuel ration. Bones were another much valued recycling commodity; collected, ground up, and sterilized, they provided much-needed additional fertilizer for field and garden alike.

SAUCEPANS FOR SPITFIRES

Metals of all sorts were particularly prized, with a separate drive for aluminium pots and pans. But this, sadly, was more symbolic than practical. The pots and pans so patriotically handed over at the beginning of the war "to make Spitfires" were, like the iron railings from outside town houses, largely the wrong grade of metal for that sort of manufacture. But people felt that they had "done their bit" and the government valued the rise in public morale, even if the aluminium was not that useful.

CHAPTER EIGHT
... AND CARRY ON